CRIME AND CRIMINALS OF VICTORIAN KENT

By Adrian Gray, M.A.

Illustrated by Tim Blake

CRIME AND CRIMINALS IN VICTORIAN KENT

By Adrian Gray, M.A.

Illustrated by Tim Blake

Meresborough Books
1985

Published by Meresborough Books, 7 Station Road, Rainham, Gillingham, Kent.
ME8 7RS.

ISBN 0905270 967

Printed in Great Britain by
Whitstable Litho Ltd., Whitstable, Kent

To Fiona and Sue, neither of whom – of course – knows anything about crime.

CONTENTS

INTRODUCTION

Until the last few years the Victorian Age has been treated as 'recent' history, since there were many alive who could still remember it. But now it seems that the values and standards of the Victorian Age are separated from the present by centuries rather than decades, how could anyone today condone such things as transportation, the workhouse and public executions? The reader who searches back into the files of Kent local newspapers for 1837-1901 will find that it was then a wholly different county from how it is today. Such investigation will also reveal that the Victorian era was far from being a 'golden age' except for the wealthy few who could dissociate themselves from ordinary life; to be less than rich in the time of Queen Victoria was to be condemned to a life of constant drudgery, fear of poverty and a certain knowledge that illness could bring the end of everything. It was in this atmosphere that crime flourished.

The 'Welfare State' did not come into being until after the First World War. For the ordinary folk of Victorian Kent this meant that the only escape – should misfortune strike in the shape of unemployment or illness – was the workhouse; this was a place considerably worse than most modern prisons. Undoubtedly a large proportion of crime in Victorian Kent was motivated by a desperate fear of this fate, so men were led to steal food and property to feed their families. Nowadays we would find it hard to condemn a man who stole meat to feed his children, let alone transport him to a distant and hostile land for the rest of his life as was the practice in the 1840s.

A large proportion of the violent assaults and murders in Victorian Kent were committed by the mentally disturbed, the most famous case being the patricide by Richard Dadd at Cobham in 1843. This also reflected the failure of Victorian England to come to terms with mental illness and the distress it could cause; little treatment was available for sufferers and the results were often tragic.

In the 1980s our press often likes to talk of 'mugging' as if it is a new social disease that has afflicted only our own age. Yet all that has changed is the terminology, for the Victorians knew the same crime as 'highway robbery'. The Dick Turpin style of robber had already vanished, but groups of 'footpads' still lurked on country roads or even on prosperous thoroughfares such as Chatham Hill; working in threes or fours, they preyed on solitary pedestrians, often using a woman as 'bait'. If anything, Victorian muggers were more sophisticated and dangerous than their modern-day counterparts.

Some crimes that were serious in Victorian England have now disappeared altogether. 'Breach of Promise' cases have vanished, and so have prosecutions for 'unnatural relations with an animal' – although the latter was always a difficult crime to 'prove'. 'Furious driving' though has merely changed from being a matter of 20mph to 70mph and 'dangerous driving' – one of the few ways in which Victorian life was considerably safer than life at present!

Overall this book will reveal that Victorian Kent was often a cruel and heartless place to live. It was a County where crowds cheered at public executions, where girls strangled their illegitimate babies at birth and where a fourteen-year-old boy could be transported to Australia for seven years after stealing a mere fifteen shillings in cash.

CHAPTER ONE

'WILFUL MURDER'

It is common in the 1980s to hear people talking about how violent daily life has become, but it is an undoubted fact that sudden death was far more common during the Victorian Age. Kent local papers of the time were regularly filled with details of violent deaths in the home, on the highway or, most commonly, around the pub. Crimes of violence were common and many of them ended with fatalities. Yet the Judges at the Kent Assizes often showed remarkable liberality in directing whether a crime should be considered 'wilful murder' or manslaughter. This was an important distinction, because murder carried a sentence of death by hanging whilst manslaughter was punished in a variety of ways – anything from a few months in prison to transportation for life.

Until the end of 1866 murderers sentenced to death were executed by being hung in public outside Maidstone gaol. After that executions took place within the prison walls and with only a few witnesses, such as the prison chaplain; the first man to be executed 'privately' was Thomas Wells, who had shot dead the stationmaster at Dover Harbour. He was executed in August 1868. Before Wells, a steady stream of men had been executed publicly at Maidstone, though on each occasion the more sober journalists in the County had condemned the unpleasant scenes. These unfortunate men were:

Samuel Seager, for murder at Otterden, exec. 28th March 1839

George Willis, for the murder of William Shepherd at Woolwich, exec. 4th July 1839

John Hutchins, for the murder of his wife at Deptford, exec. 7th October 1847

George Millen, for murder of Mr Laws at Bethersden, exec. 29th March 1849

Dedea Redanies, for murder of two sisters near Folkestone, exec. 1st January 1857

George Bowe, for murder of a corporal at Woolwich, exec. 4th June 1857

Thomas Mansell, for murder of a corporal at Dover, exec. 6th July 1857

? Edwards, for murder of his brother at Maidstone, exec. 20th August 1857

Fox, for murder of a young woman in Canterbury, exec. 20th August 1857

Frederick Prentice, for murder of a young woman at Sheerness, exec. 7th April 1859

Peter Masterson, for murder of a sergeant at Woolwich, exec. 19th September 1859

R. Burton, for murder of a boy at Chatham, exec. 11th April 1863

Holden, for murder of his child, exec. 20th August 1863

Eldridge, for murder of the Herne carrier near Canterbury, exec. 20th August 1863

John Currie, for murder of Major de Vere at Chatham, exec. 12th October 1865

Stephen Forward, alias Walter Southey, for murder of various people in London and Ramsgate, exec. January 1866

There were many cases of suspicious death that never got as far as the Assizes. In an age when 'detective work' was hardly known, the role of the Coroner was a very important one and whenever anyone died suddenly the local coroner would hold an inquest to judge how that person had died. The Coroner's court was always aware that a verdict of 'wilful murder' could end with a person being hung, and therefore extreme caution seems to have been the order of the day. Occasionally the Coroner's verdict differed from that of the general public and wild, hysterical scenes resulted; the 'Holgate Affair' in New Brompton, described later, is an example of this.

One problem that the Coroner faced was how to distinguish between deliberate murder and death caused by a brawl that got out of hand. A case at the beginning of the Victorian Age illustrates this problem. In February 1838 a group of tramps were seen fighting in the streets of Dartford and one of them, Michael Larkin, fell to the ground with a four-inch knife wound in his stomach, from which he soon died. The Coroner had the arduous task of collecting evidence as to what had happened, a job made even more difficult by the facts that Larkin had at least two other aliases and all the participants had had a great deal too much to drink! Memories were, to say the least, confused. It soon transpired that Larkin had been stabbed by Eliza Wright, a woman with whom he had been living, in the course of a row about 'another woman'. The Coroner's verdict was manslaughter since the death had occurred as a result of an argument that got out of control rather than a plan for 'wilful murder'. Wright was lucky to get off with only a year in prison.

A common type of murder involved a newly-born baby being disposed of by its mother. The usual pattern involved an unmarried girl who had successfully concealed her pregnancy and the birth, which was in itself a crime. In Plumstead in 1838 a twenty-one year old unmarried girl called Lever gave birth and then cruelly disposed of the child. The girl had kept her pregnancy secret even from her mother, though the older woman had had her suspicions. At one stage the girl 'complained to her mother of being unwell and of having had a violent pain in the bowels'. Her mother immediately suspected pregnancy, but the girl denied it. A few days later the girl gave birth whilst her mother was out. When she returned the mother guessed what had happened and challenged her daughter. The girl was at last forced to admit it and said: "I have had a child since you have been gone; it is alright, being down the privy". A policeman was called and duly found the body of a baby in the privy, concealed beneath some rubbish which had hastily been piled on top of it by the girl. She was taken off to prison.

Quite a large proportion of the murder cases in Victorian Kent involved soldiers. George Willis was based at Woolwich in 1839 and was a fairly simple man who had come under a great deal of pressure. One particular day his troubles were mounting up and he was having great difficulty in coping when he was ordered out onto parade. Whilst rushing to the parade ground he at last snapped and, in his fury, shot dead Sergeant-Major Shepherd who was taking the parade. Such an action posed a serious threat to the reliability of the armed forces and so, for Willis, there could be no mercy. He was executed in public in Maidstone in July 1839, with the usual crowd of ghouls gathered around the scaffold. The *Maidstone Journal* deplored the scene itself and the behaviour of the crowd afterwards:

> 'The melancholy scene appeared to have made very little impression upon the crowd; for, immediately after the execution, the public houses were crammed with inmates, and drinking and jollity appeared to be the only things thought of.'

Public executions were invariably greeted with heartless behaviour from the mob, many of whom travelled many miles to watch the death throes of some poor unfortunate. After his death Willis was found to have had a double row of front teeth.

Murders of Policemen were fairly rare. The Kent County Constabulary was formed in 1857 and only suffered one fatality during the Victorian period, but prior to that date the Police were a local responsibility and suffered a few losses. One of the worst incidents was at Dover in September 1844 and involved a battle between the local constables and a pub full of chimney-sweeps and prize-fighters. James Clark was an old sweep from Canterbury who had five sons who shared his trade; a number of the sons, notably Thomas, were also involved in prize-fighting and, because of this, they all turned up at Dover one day in the autumn of 1844. It was a Sunday and as the sun set a terrible storm developed and the Clark family retreated to a pub where they consumed a great deal of alcohol in the company of other prizefighting supporters. Inevitably there was trouble and two policemen arrived to sort it out. The odds were hopelessly against them and, as usual when the Police arrived to sort out a pub, previous arguments were forgotten in the enthusiasm for an assault on the 'common enemy'. Thomas Clark grabbed a broomhandle to which a piece of iron was attached and struck one of the constables across the face with it in the region of the nose. The constable, who had come unscathed through twenty-six years of service in the Marines, collapsed and died. A furious struggle ensued, after which James Clark, the old man, and some of his sons were arrested.

Thomas Clark, however, escaped and, despite a Government reward of £50 being offered, was never captured. The old man and two of his sons appeared at the Assizes in November, charged with murder. It soon became clear that the murder had been entirely Thomas' work, so his father and brothers were found 'not guilty' of murder. The appearance of the family in court excited a great deal of interest, especially as they fitted everyone's idea of what villains should look like. James Clark, the old man, had 'a low forehead, sunken eyes, and a lower jaw unusually long, the loss of his upper teeth rendering it more particularly prominent'. So most of the family were let off but, being rogues, one of the brothers was soon in trouble again; this time he was transported to Australia for stealing a cheese.

Sometimes execution was avoided because of the suicide of the murderer. This happened with the Elham murders of 1846, when a bricklayer named Sharruck Bragg killed his wife and one of his children with a hammer. In his frenzy, however, he missed the baby which was found several hours later. After committing the murders, Bragg cut his own throat. The bodies were discovered when blood, dripping through the floorboards, alerted the people living on the ground floor beneath the Bragg family. Events like this were often the direct result of a society which was very slow to understand the symptoms of mental illness, the usual victims being members of the murderer's own family.

A domestic dispute at Erith in 1893 led to a sentence of death on Henry Kelsey, which was carried out in January 1894. Kelsey's victim was a Miss Burton, with whom he had been living. The crime took place in the street in the middle of Erith, so there were plenty of witnesses. The couple were walking along the pavement when Kelsey placed an arm round Miss Burton's neck, pulled her head back and stabbed her in the throat. He then attempted to kill himself with the same knife, but failed. Kelsey's defence was to claim that she had killed herself – 'I did not kill the woman. I lent her my knife, and when I saw what she had done I said I would die with her too'. But a doctor's evidence proved that her knife-wounds could not have been self-inflicted and Kelsey paid the ultimate penalty.

Another family murder involved Thomas Jackson, a labourer from Chalk. Ill and unemployed, Jackson found the burden of bringing up a family of five children too great and, in a moment of insanity, cut the throats of two of his boys and dumped their bodies in a chalk pit at Denton. Jackson himself was found nearby, bleeding profusely from a throat wound from which he later died. Witnesses at the inquest testified to the problems that Jackson had encountered in bringing up a large family on his own with no support from 'society'. It was said that he had been a good man turned insane by worry and one witness reported that Jackson had already attempted to drown himself. It was further evidence that a large proportion of murders in Victorian Kent were not committed by heartless killers, but by people who, given some judicious and kindly assistance, might never have hurt anyone.

1 The Otterden Murder, 1839

The first man to be executed in Kent during the reign of Queen Victoria was Samuel Seager, a thirty-year-old bachelor from Otterden, a small and isolated hamlet a few miles from Charing. The events that took place there in January 1839 were typical of what could happen when tensions built up within such a small community.

In the first few weeks of 1839 a young couple by the name of Jenkins were eagerly anticipating going to a wedding. However, they had a family of small children and, as going to the wedding would take several hours, they arranged for a local woman named Hannah Giles to babysit while they were away. It had been snowing, so there was the possibility that they might be delayed in their return and the Jenkins did not want their children left alone for too long. But when the time came for them to leave, Hannah Giles had not arrived; not wishing to be late, they told their little boy that she would soon be there and quickly left for the wedding.

The little boy did not stay in the house as he had been told to do, but went out into the country lanes to see if he could see Mrs Giles hurrying towards their home. Whilst looking around he suddenly found, to his horror, a body lying beside the road. Without even stopping to find out who it was, the little boy ran straight home and locked himself into the house in a state of total fright.

Hours passed by before the Jenkins couple, returning home from the wedding, found the body of Mrs Giles cold beside the road.

A murder investigation was quickly started and there was plenty of evidence for the local magistrates. Closer investigation revealed that Mrs Giles had been shot and, for good measure, her throat had been cut. She had been shot four times and the murderer had made some attempt to disguise his crime by trying to burn the body, but he had failed. Two clues pointed to an immediate suspect, for a trail of footprints had been left in the snow and led to the house of a local man named Samuel Seager, and a pistol was found near the body.

Seager had been living with his mother and she readily identified the pistol as his. Her evidence later proved most important since she told the Coroner about how she had seen her son with the gun, had guessed that it would lead to tragedy and had unsuccessfully struggled to get it from him. Materials found in the Seager home showed that the murderer had made his own shot by casting lead into moulds hollowed out of potatoes.

The murderer had disappeared and within a few days had fled from the County, blending into the large numbers of single men who wandered the country, often alone, in those troubled times. Lacking anything to be said about the criminal, local interest instead focussed on the motive for the crime. At first the local press painted a picture of Seager as a black-hearted villain and Mrs Giles as an innocent victim. Rumours spread that Seager, a bachelor, had developed a passion for Mrs Giles but that she, a married woman, had turned him down. But early in February Seager was captured by an alert constable at Coleshill, near Birmingham, and in the trial a different picture emerged.

It became obvious that the Otterden murder resulted from the unhappy marriages and rather loose morals that were typical of isolated country districts at that time, an age when no-one would marry a woman unless she could prove her fecundity by becoming pregnant. New evidence revealed that Seager's passion for Mrs Giles was far from unrequited and that they were, in fact, 'intimate'. The dead woman was described in the *Maidstone Journal* as 'a most profligate character'. Seager tried to defend himself with an argument about how Mrs Giles had become jealous of his relationship with another married woman, and had caused him great difficulty, but he must have known that the evidence about his possession of the gun would point to a premeditated act – the capital offence of 'wilful murder'.

Seager must have known the likely verdict even before he came to trial in March 1839, for as soon as he had been arrested he had tried to strangle himself with his boot-laces whilst in gaol. Throughout the trial he behaved in a very haughty manner, but as he passed away the days before his execution his whole demeanour changed. Instead of rejecting the presence of the Chaplain, he now welcomed him and became thoroughly penitent. He was due to be executed at noon on 28th March 1839, and spent the hours of 3am to 7am that morning praying on his knees in the cell. His last comfort came when the Chaplain read Psalm 39 to him, the last verse of which is a plea that 'I may recover strength before I go hence and be no more'.

After such a repentance, it was indeed a tragedy that Seager's public execution in front of the people of Maidstone was marked by the sort of unpleasant scenes that eventually caused executions to be moved inside the prison where the general public were excluded. The execution was watched by many thousands of people, most of whom were women and children. Local journalists wondered what sort of mother brought her young family to such occasions. There was, as always, a great deal of drinking and brawling. Seager's appearance and death were greeted with shouts of laughter, often mixed with cruel and vicious comments. Right at the front of the baying mob was Hannah Giles' husband, a man who by all accounts was of no high moral standards himself. After Seager was dead, Giles stayed on to gloat over the body which was gently swaying in the breeze; 'Him, he looks better now than I ever see him in his life', was Giles' last comment on the body of the man who had killed his wife.

The Otterden murder was a sad case wholly typical of the rural murders of the period, where isolated and enclosed communities created a hothouse atmosphere in which feelings ran high and often led to violence.

2 The Famous Artist who Murdered His Father, Cobham 1843

In the early autumn of 1843 the body of a murdered man was found in Lord Darnley's park at Cobham. This was the start of one of the most sensational murder cases of the Victorian era, involving a young man with an unbalanced mind who had already established himself as an artist and whose pictures are, today, worth hundreds of thousands of pounds.

Mr Charles Dadd was a local man and had at one time been a chemist in Rochester. As his career, and the size of his family, developed he moved up to London and lived at Suffolk Street. In London, Charles Dadd achieved some commercial success after inventing a form of improved oil for use by artists; perhaps because of the family interest in art, Dadd's third son, Richard, was encouraged in his skill for painting and began submitting pictures for exhibition at the Royal Academy whilst still a very young man. As part of his training, young Richard Dadd went abroad in 1842-3 and visited many famous sites in the

Mediterranean and the Middle East. Throughout the trip he worked at his painting with an almost obsessive compulsion and, very soon after his return, it became obvious that Richard Dadd was 'labouring under aberration of intellect'.

The study of mental illness was far from scientific at this time and doctors were only able to advance vague guesses at the cause of Richard Dadd's illness. It was generally held that he was suffering from 'softening of the brain', which doctors believed had been caused by 'arduous study and constant exposure to the sun'. Charles Dadd, however, was clearly a devoted father and did not abandon his son, although doctors warned him that Richard might become dangerous; this devotion was to cost Mr Dadd very dearly.

Towards the end of August 1843 father and son planned an expedition into Kent together. Living in London they had heard about the plans to stage massive Army manoeuvres at Chatham and the pair decided to go down to Kent to watch these unusually grand events. For some unknown reason, Richard saw this as an opportunity to kill his father and prepared for the trip by going to Covent Garden and buying a flick-knife with an eight-inch blade and a cut-throat razor.

From the subsequent events it is quite clear that Richard had made a definite decision to murder his father and influenced their plans for the trip to gain himself the right opportunity. The normal route to Chatham would have been straight down the River Thames by steamer, or along the railway through Gravesend. But, under his son's influence, Charles Dadd took Richard from Gravesend to Cobham – well off the direct route, though he was well-known in Cobham from his days as a local chemist.

The pair of men arrived in Cobham, paid for a room at a local inn and had a meal. It was a beautifully peaceful and sunny evening, typical of the last few days of summer when August and September join. Richard Dadd, clearly plotting the murder with great care, suggested an evening walk.

Neither of the two men returned to their Cobham inn. The next morning a Rochester butcher, Abraham Lyster, was travelling through Lord Darnley's park (which was at the time let to William Lake) when he noticed a man slumped in the grass. His first reaction was that the man was just another drunk, sleeping off the worst excesses of a heavy night. But from his clothes Lyster could tell that the man was a gentleman and so stopped to investigate. He turned the man over, since he was lying face-down, and was horrified to find bloody wounds in the neck and left breast. He immediately ran for a constable and alerted some of the Cobham estate workers.

An investigation of the body and the surrounding area started as soon as the local constable arrived. There seemed two immediate possibilities – that the gentleman had been murdered by a thief, or that he had committed suicide – but evidence soon showed that neither was the case. A search of the dead man's pockets revealed a gold watch and three sovereigns, so it could not have been a vicious robbery. A number of factors indicated that it was not suicide – the victim's coat had been pulled over his head after his throat had been cut and before he had been stabbed in the chest, the grass in the area had been crushed flat as if in a desperate struggle and there were footmarks of two people. One of the murder weapons, the knife, was found thirteen yards from the body, where it could not have been thrown by a dying man, and underneath the corpse was a cut-throat razor smeared with blood. The constable had all the evidence of murder by an unknown person, but no suggestion whatsoever of a possible motive.

Only when the body was taken back to Cobham and placed in the 'Ship Inn' did the constable begin to make any progress in his enquiries. A waiter there recognised the body as that of a man who had taken tea at the inn the previous day, in the company of a rather strange young man. It took no time at all after that to identify the body of Charles Dadd and to institute a search for his son, Richard.

The next few days revealed a report that Richard Dadd had been seen in London, asking questions about how to get to France, but after that the trail went cold. In fact France was exactly where Dadd had gone, though his first action after the murder had been to make for Rochester where he stopped off at the 'Crown Inn' only briefly in order to wash the blood from his hands. He stole the towel from the inn as he had smeared it with blood, but left blood on the handbasin; the maid at the inn cleaned the basin out without realising that it was blood that had made such a mess of it. After a brief return to London Dadd hurried to Dover where he hired a boat to take him over the English Channel for £10. Then he disappeared into the interior of France.

Had Richard Dadd been a sane and rational man, he might well have evaded the authorities for good. However, the mental illness that had caused him to murder his father reasserted itself whilst in France; whilst travelling by coach near Fontainebleu, Dadd attacked another passenger but this time was overpowered and arrested. The French authorities soon realised that they had an English lunatic on their hands and Dadd was transferred to an asylum near Beauvais where he spent many hours conversing with an imaginary person.

It was his family's wish that Dadd should stay in the French asylum where he could expect reasonable care, whereas in England lunatics were poorly catered for. However, an officer from the Metropolitan Police was sent to France to collect Dadd and bring him back for trial at the Kent Assizes on a charge of murdering his father. There were no reports of any difficulties in getting Dadd back to Britain, though it was said that he spent an hour of every day staring into the sun. He arrived back in England in March 1844; the press was generally sympathetic towards him, commenting that he was expected to die shortly and also reporting that mental illness had destroyed his ability to paint – neither of these claims proved to be even remotely true!

Had Dadd been sane he would have been executed, but the law allowed for a lunatic to be given over to medical authorities instead of paying the capital penalty. When Richard Dadd appeared before the magistrates in Rochester, it became immediately evident that his mind was very unbalanced indeed, so much so that the magistrates' court threatened to turn into a comedy theatre! Richard Dadd constantly interrupted the proceedings and proved himself to be a skilful mimic, imitating the magistrates so far as to inform the witnesses 'you may go out' etc. At frequent intervals he would burst into irrational outpourings of words and at other times would appear to be talking to an invisible friend. One of his speeches was reported by the *Maidstone Journal*: 'I tell you I didn't do it; no gammon about it; no. I shan't do it; I dare say; I can say; I shan't do that; I never did it, I tell you; oh gammon; I know sir.'

Richard Dadd was certified insane at the Kent Assizes in autumn 1844 and spent the rest of his life under medical supervision. He did not, as predicted, die early, but lived well into old age. Nor did his artistic skills desert him, for he was lucky enough to have an enlightened doctor who saw the encouragement of his art as Dadd's only chance to escape from his illness. The result was that Richard Dadd blossomed into one of the finest artists of the Victorian era. His masterpiece, *Oberon and Titania*, took him many years to complete, and is now valued in the salerooms at over a million pounds. But Dadd was lucky, for very few criminal lunatics could have expected any treatment even remotely comparable in humanity to that Richard Dadd received.

3 The Redanies Case – Folkestone, 1856

Most murders in which soldiers played a part involved the death of a superior officer or a bout of heavy drinking. The murders committed by Swiss-born Dedea Redanies at Capel-le-Ferne, near Folkestone, were different from both of these, for they were the traditional 'crime of passion'.

Redanies was a soldier in the British Swiss Legion, based at Shorncliffe Barracks near Folkestone. One of his mundane duties was to take the regimental laundry to Dover, where it was washed by a Mrs Back. This cannot have been too arduous a task for Redanies, since Mrs Back possessed two assets of great interest to any soldier – a brace of teenage daughters. It was not long before Redanies became a close friend of the elder daughter, eighteen-year-old Caroline. They 'walked out together' on many occasions in 1856 and, in due course, Caroline told Redanies that she was pregnant.

One evening Redanies asked Caroline if she would walk to Shorncliffe with him to meet his sister and it became obvious that Redanies wanted her to do this as a preliminary to getting married. Mrs Back, however, seems to have been a stern woman and would not let Caroline go off with a man to such a place; she did agree, though, that they could go in the morning providing that they took the younger sister, Maria, as a 'chaperone'.

The three of them set off in the very early morning on 3rd August 1856, planning to walk the few miles to the Camp before the day got too warm. This was the last Mrs Back saw of her daughters, for later that day their bodies were found at a place called 'Steddy Hole' near Capel-le-Ferne; they had been stabbed and their throats cut with a knife. Redanies was not to be seen, nor had he reported back to Camp.

At first no-one knew why Redanies had committed such apparently senseless murders, especially that of the girl everyone had thought he was in love with.

However, his escape route took him through Lower Hardres where he posted two letters – one to his commanding officer and another to Mrs Back. The latter was a confused and distraught attempt to explain why he had murdered the girls. He claimed that Caroline had been deceiving him and was not pregnant as she had at one time claimed. They had had a row and she had given him his portrait back – a symbol of rejection. In fury he had thrown it into the fireplace where it had smashed. Despite all this, he claimed in his letter, he still loved her but was convinced she intended to run off to Woolwich with another soldier; the thought of losing her to another man was too much and he had resolved to kill Caroline.

The walk to Shorncliffe had seemed the perfect opportunity and he had bought a dagger in Dover on 2nd August in order to be ready for his chance. Throughout his trial he denied that he had murdered Maria, having said in his letter that 'she got in the way' when he attacked Caroline. Redanies painted a dramatic picture of the last moments of his girlfriend, saying that after he had stabbed her he 'rushed over her and gave her the last kiss as an everlasting embrace'.

Redanies' attempt to escape the Police was not very successful since he was spotted by a Constable near Canterbury and, after a struggle, was arrested. In the melée he stabbed himself with the dagger, but soon recovered from the wound after a stay in hospital under guard. Damning evidence was found on him at the time of arrest, since he was carrying articles of clothing that belonged to the dead girls.

The trial of Redanies at the Kent Winter Assizes in 1856 was made complicated by his poor command of English, so an interpreter had to be arranged. He admitted the murder of Caroline, but denied that of Maria. There was too much evidence of premeditation for Redanies to escape a 'guilty' verdict and the death penalty, but his case also ran into trouble when no independent witnesses could support Redanies' argument that he had had a row with Caroline. Why had she been prepared to go to Shorncliffe with him if they had fallen out with each other? Redanies' case clearly was far from watertight and he was executed at Maidstone on 1st January 1857.

4 The Mass-Murderer from Ramsgate, 1865

Without a doubt the most extraordinary murderer in Victorian Kent was a young man from Ramsgate who was known as Ernest Walter Southey or Stephen Forward, (also spelt 'Forwood') according to which of his two lives he was living at the time. His case was all the more sensational because of the number of his victims and his denunciation of certain leading figures in Victorian England who he said had contributed to his crimes: the Bishop of London, the Earl of Dudley and Lord Palmerston were all named at his trial. In his last moments various Kent people tried to rescue Forward by applying to the Secretary of State to have his sentence of death altered since he was a lunatic, but Dr Kirkman of the County Lunatic Asylum could find no evidence to suggest that Forward was mad. Perhaps his story suggests otherwise.

Stephen Forward's origins are shrouded in mystery since we only have his own account to go by. He claimed that he was born in Ramsgate at about the time England was recovering from the strain of the Napoleonic Wars. Forward claimed that his father was a smuggler and his mother a laundress, living at Saint Lawrence. These humble origins may have been fanciful, since Forward's early life did not indicate any particular poverty such as was always a problem for washerwomen. His mother died when he was thirteen and he inherited £120, which he was apparently not able to use since he became a page boy for a while.

In his mid-teenage years several important influences came to bear on Forward's life. He was apprenticed to a baker in Ramsgate and, during his time there, met a girl called Mary, who was later to become his wife and – eventually – one of his victims. He also become a follower of a sect called the 'Faulknerites', a group who held 'hyper-Calvinistic' views such as a rigid belief in the doctrine of predestination.

After a few more years Stephen Forward married Mary and her family, who evidently possessed considerable resources, set him up with his own baking business in Ramsgate. This should have provided the Forwards with a steady income of £400 per year, but it was at this stage that Forward's fatal weaknesses began to emerge. Later he blamed his slide into ruin on his wife who, he said, had a 'cold temperament'. At any rate, he was unfaithful to his wife after only seven months of marriage. He also wrote that at this time he became a victim of 'vice'; on the exact nature of this vice contemporary sources are very vague, though they do say that it affected Stephen Forward's mind, so he may well have contracted syphilis as a result of his marital infidelities. At the same time he lost his religious faith and abandoned the Faulknerites.

After only fifteen months of marriage the baking business failed and Forward was left with no means of supporting his wife and child. His solution was to take the first step on the road to becoming a drifter by going to London in search of a job. At first he thought that he had a chance of a clerical job with the South Eastern Railway, but this fell through and he went back to being a journeyman-baker. His restless temperament showed through, however, and he quickly switched jobs and became a travelling salesman dealing in rope. For a while his wife and child joined him in London, but they became ill and had to spend some time in hospital before eventually returning to Ramsgate. Lacking solid domestic ties he launched out on the downward slope that ended with his trial as a mass-murderer.

Two things seem certain about Stephen Forward. He possessed a very restless personality that made it difficult for him to settle to any one task, and he was a disastrous businessman. His venture into commerce and the rope trade culminated in debts of £1,800, for which in those days it was still possible to be imprisoned. Instead Forward absconded, running off to try to start a new life elsewhere just as he had done after the collapse of the bakery business.

He went first to Bristol, where it was his original intention to sail for America, and then to Bath. Whilst in the west he began to frequent billiard rooms, then popular because of the unbridled gambling opportunities they offered. At first Forward was totally ignorant of billiards, but when he started to play he found that he had a talent for the game which he could turn into profit through betting. This allowed him to eke out an uncertain living before, in May 1857, he went to Liverpool.

According to his own account, Forward never neglected his family and sent money to Ramsgate whenever he could. Whilst in Liverpool he wrote to his wife and told her to advertise any reply in the newspapers since he was still afraid of being arrested for debt. After Liverpool he moved on to Dublin and then to Glasgow, in each place slipping further and further into destitution. Glasgow was the bottom rung of the ladder and for a while he slept out in the streets and begged for food.

But Forward's luck was not always bad and, through his experience with the billiard tables, he was able to get a job in Glasgow running some billiard rooms. He did well enough at this to move on to be in charge of a new yacht club, but then his old problems of temperament reasserted themselves and he began to drift once more.

Forward ended up in Brighton in 1862, a pleasure resort that offered many opportunities for winning money on the billiards tables. At this time he also began to form a determination to win back at least £1,800, so that he could repay his old debts, and he became obsessed with winning as much money as possible. In the winter of 1862 he was walking through Brighton near the seafront and noticed a young woman with a very desperate and sad expression making towards the pier. Forward, or Southey as he was now calling himself because of his earlier debts, gained the woman's attention and immediately found her fascinating. Her appearance was genteel, but he learnt that she was about to commit suicide. It was the start of a disastrous relationship for both parties.

Mrs White was a young mother with four children. Her husband, a teacher, had left her and her school was running into debt so that she had resolved to end her problems with suicide. Evidently she was also a very unstable woman. 'Southey' became immediately interested in her 'cause' and visited numerous clergymen in the district in an effort to raise money for her, with little success; he also took a more personal interest in her, formed an 'immoral connection' and moved in with her and her children. Southey resolved that he would work to clear not only his own debts but also those of Mrs White – but a union of two unstable people was hardly likely to bring success.

In February 1863 Southey had begun to make a little progress when he had a spectacular success. His savings now amounted to £150 but then, in one night, he won £1,172 from the Honourable Dudley Ward – the younger brother of the Earl of Dudley and an inveterate gambler. Ward had run up spectacular gambling debts in the past and on each occasion his brother had met them in order to protect the family name from disgrace. Ward now told Southey to apply to his brother for the money.

However, the Earl of Dudley had had enough; he decided that the time had come when he would no longer meet the ruinous debts and charges his prodigal brother was running up. Southey was left in despair, his one hope of meeting his own debts rapidly disappearing. By July 1863 the couple, who were now openly living together, were both becoming suicidal once more; Southey had a hare-brained scheme that, by killing themselves, he and Mrs White would cause a public sensation and a subscription would be started for the benefit of the four children, but the idea was put aside for the time being. Through 1864 Southey, trailing Mrs White and her family, drifted once more – living for a while in Surbiton and then moving to Worcester, all the time earning a living on the billiards tables.

In May 1864, having sent a number of fruitless letters to the Earl of Dudley, Southey decided on a new course of action. Mrs White was sent to visit the Earl of Dudley and gained entrance to his mansion on false pretences; once inside, though, the reason for her visit became evident and she was summarily ejected. This event led Southey to bring an action against the Earl of Dudley for assaulting Mrs White, but all he achieved was the loss of more money, though the case did achieve some publicity for him.

From August 1864 until June 1865 Southey and Mrs White lived in Putney. With obsessive zeal Southey threw himself into his campaign to recover money that he felt was rightfully his – which, it must be said, it really was since it had been won in fair and reasonable gambling. His method of campaign was to write voluminous letters to numerous dignitaries; the Bishop of London, for example, received a letter 68 pages long. Throughout this time he persistently dogged the Earl, turning up whenever the Earl of Dudley appeared in public.

In June 1865 Southey tailed Dudley Ward to Paris, pestering him about the debt without success. When he returned to Putney, Mrs White and her children had gone.

The story of Southey and Mrs White then becomes rather confused. It was clearly Mrs White's intention to depart for Australia, with her children, in August to start a new life. When Southey got back from France, though, the children were not with their mother but with their father, William White. On a Sunday night at the beginning of August 1865 Southey went to see White and collected the children from him, giving their father the impression that Southey would be accompanying them on the trip to Australia. White lived in Holborn where he was a schoolmaster and, having collected the children from him, Southey took them only as far as a coffee-house nearby.

This coffee-house was the *Star* and Southey arranged rooms there for the three children (aged six, eight and ten) and himself. Staff at the coffee-house observed that Southey went in and out a great deal during the course of his stay there with the children, but after the Tuesday evening no-one saw any more of him. On the Wednesday morning a chambermaid opened the door of the children's bedroom and found all three dead in bed. The Police soon arrived and found some suspicious bottles in the room; investigation proved that the children had each been killed with a spoonful of Prussic Acid on the Tuesday night.

Why had Southey murdered the three children? It seems that he was motivated by two things. Firstly, his failure to produce the money that was owed to him meant that he was unable to provide for Mrs White and the children in the way he desired. Secondly, and probably linked with this in his mind, Mrs White had decided to take the children to Australia and leave him behind – failure and rejection were staring him in the face once more.

The Metropolitan Police issued detailed descriptions of Southey, which were circulated throughout the country, including to the Kent County Constabulary. It did not take long for the murderer to be apprehended, since on the following Thursday he was brought before Ramsgate magistrates – under the name of Stephen Forward – and there charged with two other murders. Forward had stunned the court by announcing that he had also murdered three children in Holborn. Thus did Stephen Forward, alias Ernest Southey, return home in sensational manner.

What had happened to 'Southey' or 'Forward' between the poisoning of the White children on the Tuesday night and his appearance in the Magistrates' Court at Ramsgate on Thursday at noon? It seems that he had managed to travel undetected to Ramsgate on the Wednesday, having presumably left London before the discovery of the dead children. In Ramsgate he checked in at the *Camden Arms* and employed a local porter to trace his wife, Mrs Forward, whom he had left about eight years previously, though she had continued to receive letters and occasionally money from him. It did not take the porter long to inform him where his wife and daughter were to be found and, on the Wednesday evening, Forward set out to meet them.

It must have been quite a shock for Mrs Forward to open her door and find her long-absent husband standing there. She was clearly suspicious of his motives, for she would not let him into the house. He suggested that they go for a walk together, but she would only consent to go with him to a house in King Street that belonged to a dyer named Ellis; Mrs Forward clearly felt safer in the presence of others. Ellis left the room so that they could talk but remained in the vicinity. It was getting late, so Forward arranged to meet his wife at Ellis's house at eight o'clock on Thursday morning. He was invited for breakfast, but declined the offer.

Forward arrived about twenty minutes late the next morning, but he and his wife went upstairs in Ellis's house to talk privately. A little while later their daughter went up to join them. All was quiet for some time and Ellis went out to work, leaving only his own daughter actually inside the house. Neither of the Ellises was quite clear who the strange visitor was, since Forward was calling himself by his adopted name of Ernest Walter Southey.

Suddenly Miss Ellis, working downstairs, was startled by the sound of a gun-shot from above. She rushed through to the stairway and was horrified to find the Forwards' child rolling down the stairs, bleeding profusely. The girl stepped back in terror, then ran to get her father who was nearby. Before either of them returned there was another gunshot. Ellis raced up the stairs and was just in time to see Mrs Forward falling to the floor, bleeding from the head. Ellis must have expected a struggle but the strange visitor simply handed over the pistol and readily submitted to arrest. It was as if he had finished with life, his purpose exhausted.

But for the town of Ramsgate the sensations were only just starting. Forward was hauled before the local magistrates at noon and stunned them by announcing that he had left three little children lying dead in London. He made no attempt to cover up his crimes but instead placed the moral blame upon other shoulders – he denounced Palmerston, Stanley, Sir Richard Mayne, the Earl of Derby, the Honourable Edward Bulwer-Lytton, the Bishop of London, Gladstone, Disraeli and the Earl of Shaftesbury; presumably all these people had failed to reply to his letter about the Earl of Dudley's debts.

There was some confusion over Forward's identity. He had arrived in Ramsgate sporting spectacles and a false beard but, when these were removed, several people were able to recognise him as the Stephen Forward who had once been a baker in the town. Yet he insisted that he should be called Southey and refused to answer any questions addressed to him under his old name. After his appearance in the Magistrates' Court Forward (or Southey!) was taken to Sandwich gaol to await trial; there, on 10th August, he wrote a long and densely-argued statement blaming his crimes on the Church and the State who, he said, had ignored his desperate pleas for help. There was some truth in this, for Forward had frequently threatened to kill the children or commit suicide but had always been ignored as a harmless crank. The Earl of Dudley had also dismissed him as a weak and powerless character and the failure to raise the money was the reason Forward gave for having killed the children. Forward was not a hardened criminal, but a desperately confused and inadequate man who had – for years – been crying out for help.

Nonetheless he was tried at Maidstone in December 1865 on a charge of wilfully murdering Mary Forward, his wife, and Emily, his daughter. Even his appearance at the trial in Maidstone had caused some controversy, for the Metropolitan Police had wanted him to be tried in London for the murder of the White children – but the Kent authorities claimed right of possession and he was tried for his second batch of murders.

The trial started, predictably enough, with a wrangle between the defendant and the Judge over what he was to be called. The charges were made out against Forward, but the prisoner insisted that he was Southey. The Judge wisely decided that a name made little real difference if the prisoner admitted the murders anyway, so 'Southey' became his official name at last. He came prepared for the trial, carrying a huge bundle of papers which consisted mostly of his various letters on the subject of the gambling debt. Southey was charged initially with the murder of Mary Forward, which he denied on the grounds that she was already dead when he shot her; this was not a successful defence and he was found guilty, with a sentence of death.

Southey regarded his trial fatalistically, seemingly relieved that he was going to die. He constantly interrupted proceedings by shouting out that 'Man's justice is a mockery, but thank God that I am going out of this world'. This gave some local philanthropists hope that his life would be spared on the grounds of insanity, but there was not enough evidence of an unsound mind to satisfy the Secretary of State. In the three weeks between his sentence and his execution, Southey continued to maintain that the real blame lay with the Earl of Dudley and 'society'. But as 1865 drew to a close his protests still fell on deaf ears.

Southey was due to be hanged in the middle of January 1866. On his last Sunday he broke down and confessed fully to his crimes, accepting the moral as well as the actual blame – presumably much to the Earl of Dudley's relief. Southey wrote:

> 'I desire to acknowledge openly that the overwhelming mass of troubles to which I have been subjected, and which have been the means of bringing me to a sad and untimely end, are closely traceable to my having lost in my earlier years the guiding and soothing belief of the truths of the Christian religion. And I desire to acknowledge before all men my heartfelt and deeply sorrowful sense of my utter sinfulness.'

Despite this, Southey still held that he had done the right thing in committing the murders.

Southey was one of the last people to be executed in public, but the event was much quieter than on previous occasions. New rules had been introduced to make executions less of a spectacle, so the crowds were no longer interested. The *Maidstone Journal* described his last moments:

> '. . . The scaffold was hung round with black cloth to such a height that when the drop fell only just the top of the convict's head was visible to the crowd. The body, after hanging an hour, was cut down and a cast of the head taken. In the afternoon the body was buried within the precincts of the gaol.'

And so ended the short and sad life of Stephen Forward, a man who, because of his inadequacies, murdered four children and a young woman. The Secretary of State judged that he was sane enough to stand trial and be executed for 'Wilful Murder', in other words that he rationally premeditated the death of these people. The facts must speak for themselves.

5 The Mad Woman of Tunbridge Wells, 1866

Mental illness was still a largely unexplored problem in Victorian times and confused social relationships often placed a great strain on the mentally disturbed. This was particularly the case amongst the lower classes where marital relations were often rather 'fluid' and where evidence of mental instability was generally ignored for years. Such was the case with Ann Lawrence.

By all accounts Ann Lawrence had a disturbed childhood. When she was young she lived at Farningham, but her mother died and her father could not be bothered to look after her, so she was thrown out. Most of her teenage years she spent living with an older cousin named Walter Higham, during which time an affection developed between the two of them as she matured into an attractive young woman. This did not go unnoticed by Higham's wife, with the result that Ann was thrown out yet again. This time Ann went to Maidstone, where she married and, in 1862, gave birth to a child that she named Jeremiah.

In 1863 Ann met up with Walter Higham again and this time they formed a more permanent relationship. Both abandoned their previous marriage partners and set up home in Tunbridge Wells, where Higham got work as a vegetable hawker. Ann brought little Jeremiah with her.

The couple lived together in reasonable peace until early 1866, when Ann began to form certain suspicions about Walter's behaviour. She accused him of having another woman in Malling, which he denied. Neighbours observed that Ann had a fierce temper. Then, one night in June 1866, she borrowed a bill-hook from a neighbour in order to chop some wood.

The couple went to bed quite normally that night, but at five o'clock the next morning Higham was woken up by sudden and intense pain. He awoke to see his lover, Ann, kneeling above him and wielding the bill-hook. Higham was too dazed to react immediately, but managed to ward off blows to his face by putting his arms in the way, as a result of which he received some severe lacerations. Higham managed to get out of the bed and made a dash for the door, hoping to get out into the street and so gain safety. But he slipped and Ann caught him up; passers-by in the street saw her bashing his head against the wall before he finally managed to escape into another house.

Thwarted in her attempt to kill her lover, Ann Lawrence turned her savage anger against her sleeping child. She grabbed Higham's razor and plunged it into the child's throat, not even pausing to remove it afterwards; the razor was still embedded there when a Policeman arrived to survey the dreadful scene some minutes later.

Having brutally killed little Jeremiah, Ann herself now rushed out into the street and started shouting at a woman who lived nearby. 'He has killed the child,' she shrieked, 'it was not his, and he never liked it.' Clearly she intended to blame her lover for the murder, but her mind was so confused that she was unable to stick to a coherent story.

Meanwhile the neighbours had run for the Police and the first Constable to arrive had no difficulty in identifying the murderess since she was spattered with the blood of her lover and her child. By this stage she was not worried about being arrested, but only wanted to vent the anger she felt for Higham. 'All he has got I gave him,' she told the Constable, 'I meant to have killed him and am sorry I did not.' Higham, desperately wounded, had already been taken to hospital.

The Constable ventured into the house and a most gruesome scene presented itself. A local newspaper reporter also visited the house shortly afterwards and

Ann Lawrence attacking her lover, Walter Higham, at Tunbridge Wells

reported that 'The room itself presented a fearful aspect; the floor, walls and even ceiling being spattered and smeared with blood'.

A Coroner's inquest was held later that day. As Higham was badly wounded he could not be moved from the hospital, but his presence was necessary since he was a principal witness. So the Coroner's Court was held at his bedside in the hospital and Ann Lawrence was taken there under close guard. A large crowd gathered outside the hospital, anxious to catch a glimpse of this dangerous woman. During the whole inquest Ann Lawrence stood in the hospital ward smiling cheerfully; when asked why she seemed so happy, she replied that it was a pleasure to see Higham so badly injured, but she would have preferred to have killed him. Under the circumstances the Coroner could do little else other than conclude that Jeremiah Lawrence had been wilfully murdered by his mother and she was sent for trial at the Assizes.

Ann Lawrence was duly found guilty of murder and sentenced to death, but this was commuted to life imprisonment. Throughout her trial she insisted that she had attacked her lover because he intended to desert her for another woman, but it was of course the evidence of her attack on the child that was crucial.

6 Two 'Murders' That Were Not

When a person dies suddenly or in suspicious circumstances, there can be two forms of trial that result: trial by way of legitimate legal processes or trial by popular opinion. In the 1980s we are still familiar with the scene of a baying mob outside a courtroom as a suspect is quickly whisked away, his head shrouded beneath a blanket. This sort of scene was common in Victorian Kent, particularly as a possible death penalty tended to lead some coroners into being reluctant to reach a verdict of 'wilful murder' if there were any doubts whatsoever.

In January 1843, in the village of Brenchley, a man by the name of Diprose suddenly became ill, started vomiting and died soon afterwards. The circumstances of his death pointed to a poisoning and the villagers rapidly came to the conclusion that the poor man had been murdered by his wife. Mrs Diprose was known to have a great fascination for the opposite sex, thereby suggesting a motive. The villagers concluded that she had killed her husband in order to free herself for another man.

Diprose's death was investigated by the local Coroner in due course. He may well have had his suspicions about the death, but unlike public opinion he had to base his findings on the evidence. There was no evidence to suggest that Diprose had been poisoned, indeed no-one seemed quite certain what had killed him. The Coroner therefore recorded an open verdict, thus incensing the Brenchley villagers.

Mrs Diprose received some rough treatment for a few days, but the affair was gradually forgotten as the winter merged into spring. But then Mrs Diprose made a mistake. She had focussed her amorous attentions on one particular man named Russell and, in April 1843, the villagers learnt that she was planning to marry him. This seemed to confirm the worst suspicions of the Brenchley people.

The result was an exceedingly unpleasant week for the widow as the villagers attempted to hound her out of her home. Every night for a week they gathered outside her house at Matfield Green, near Brenchley, between the hours of 8pm and midnight. There they set up a bizarre orchestra, ringing bells, beating kettles and tin trays, anything that would contribute to a furious din. When Mrs Diprose sought refuge in the local pub the mob followed her there. In the end they invaded her cottage's garden and there, in front of her eyes, burnt two effigies of her.

By this time Mrs Diprose was afraid that they meant to kill her and, quite sensibly, summoned the local Constable. The result was that several people were arrested and charged with assault, for which they were fined five shillings each. This did the job and after that Mrs Diprose was allowed to settle down quietly and get married, though she was still ostracised.

Unfortunately the story did not end there, for Mrs Russell, as she had now become, did not find happiness. In May 1846 she was rescued in the nick of time as she attempted to hang herself in her cottage at Matfield Green. So, having nearly died at the hands of a lynch-mob, she then nearly died by her own hand.

The 'Holgate Affair' occupied the attention of the Medway Towns for several months in 1894. This case was unusual in that a man was 'tried' by public opinion and only after that brought before a court of law.

This affair first reached the attention of the general public when a woman from New Brompton, Grace Holgate, arrived at the Medway Union workhouse one dawn in a state of considerable agitation. No sooner had she crossed the threshold than she gave birth to a child, collapsed, and died. An investigation of her body soon revealed considerable bruising.

The news quickly spread through New Brompton. As it travelled rumours about Joseph Holgate's behaviour were listened to avidly. There were many tales about rows between the couple and about occasions on which Mrs Holgate had fled from the house in fear for her life; one man, Mr Dixon, actually said that he had gone to their house after hearing screams and had arrived to find Holgate with his hands round his wife's throat.

There was little else to talk about in the Medway towns in August 1894 and the Holgate case soon took on the status of a sensation. Fact and fancy were hard to separate, but it was reported that the couple had been married for five years during which they had lived at 7 Copenhagen Road, New Brompton. Gradually, solid evidence about Holgate's attacks on his wife emerged and it was discovered that the evening before her death Grace Holgate had attempted to seek refuge at her stepfather's house, but her husband had followed her and brought her back. The next morning she was dead.

The locals, especially the women, concluded that Holgate had deliberately beaten his wife to death. A crowd of well over two hundred people, almost entirely women, turned up for the funeral and 'hooted' Holgate as soon as he arrived in the cemetery. The funeral service was constantly interrupted by their noise and on several occasions the vicar had to plead for quiet so that he could proceed. As soon as the coffin had been lowered into the ground, Holgate was pelted with a barrage of stones and sand which also hit the vicar and the mourners and injured the undertaker Mr Beveridge.

Holgate tried to slip out of the cemetery but he was spotted by the crowd and chased down Rochester High Street, where flour was thrown at him. He attempted to hide in the *Railway Hotel*, but was turned out because of the danger to the property. In the end he fled to Rochester Police Station for protection but there, to add insult to injury, he was promptly charged with having assaulted his wife and arrested. But at least he was safe from the mob.

Meanwhile events were also attracting interest at 7 Copenhagen Road. A dealer had arrived to clear the house and, sensing an opportunity for unexpected profit, held an impromptu street auction. A crowd of curious women had gathered, and the dealer was able to sell virtually anything connected with the dead woman to these ghouls; Grace Holgate's kitchen utensils sold particularly well.

The Coroner's verdict was that Grace Holgate had died through manslaughter. In early September though, additional medical evidence was produced to suggest that she died because of an attack of a rare type of fit associated with women in childbirth; had she not been in labour, Holgate's assault would not have killed her. For a while it looked as if Holgate would get off with a charge of wounding and grievous bodily harm, but the evidence of repeated assaults on his wife counted against him. In November 1894 he was found guilty of manslaughter and sentenced to ten years penal servitude. It was no more than he deserved, for all the witnesses stated that he had given his wife five years of the utmost misery which he had terminated only by killing her. On this occasion public opinion had reached the correct verdict.

CHAPTER TWO

MANSLAUGHTER

1 Sudden Death

The distinction between 'Wilful Murder' and 'Manslaughter' was very important to a Victorian jury, since the former carried an automatic death penalty and the latter did not. 'Manslaughter' came to be applied to virtually all crimes where death resulted, providing there was no evidence of the crime being premeditated. Thus many men who launched barbaric and murderous assaults on other people escaped with sentences of penal servitude or transportation. A very high proportion of deaths by manslaughter were associated with heavy drinking.

One unusual manslaughter trial resulted from an incident in Cranbrook in March 1838. William Knight, who lived at Kennardington, set out one afternoon to walk the sixteen miles to Cranbrook in order to give three wild fowls to Samuel Kennard who lived there. Knight did not arrive until ten o'clock at night and found that, after knocking heavily on the front door, he could not raise anyone from the house. He gave up with the front door and walked round the side of the house where, without warning, he was blasted by a shotgun and killed. Kennard was immediately arrested and claimed that he had been much persecuted by people banging on his door and then running away, but it was noted that he smelt heavily of drink at the time of the incident. Kennard, who was sixty-four, was found guilty of manslaughter and transported for the remainder of his life.

Sometimes the Victorian legal system proved to be merciful. Another incident in 1838 occurred at Boughton Monchelsea, where William Wickings was responsible for the death of William Cork. It appeared that the two youths had been larking around with a whip; Wickings had flicked it and Cork had fallen down dead. The High Sheriff of Kent intervened to give Wickings a character reference, declaring that he was 'of very weak intellect'. He was punished with one month in prison and a fine of one shilling.

A verdict of manslaughter was usually attached to deaths which resulted from an argument turning into a fight. An example of this was in Chatham in 1840 when Edward Thomas stabbed and killed John Grigg in the course of an argument. The row was about buying clothes from soldiers, a practice which was also illegal; soldiers were induced to sell items of their kit for cash, but on their subsequent return to barracks were liable to be punished – the end result tended to be that they absconded.

A highly typical manslaughter case involving drink occurred at Smarden in May 1840. An unemployed sweep named Bell was passing through the village in a quest for work and stopped at an inn where he joined a group of locals who were gambling. Inevitably the gamblers started cheating Bell, who was the only outsider present, and a fight started. The Smarden locals easily overpowered the

The fight between Pearce and his wife

itinerant sweep, knocked him down and put him under a settle in the bar. To make matters worse they stole his bag and poor Bell could not discover which of the troublemakers had removed it. Bell went to find a constable to help him but there was not one about and, when he returned to the inn on his own, he was promptly thrown out into the street. By this time Bell was seething with anger and frustration, so he went to a nearby shop and bought a clasp knife for six pence. With this in his hand he returned to the inn and stabbed one of his tormentors, Munns. Despite the high degree of provocation involved, Bell was punished severely and transported for life.

One man who got away more easily was William Pearce of Chelsfield. Pearce had a common-law wife with a rather fiery temperament and, in October 1840, this flared up into a spectacular row. The woman had drunk three pints of beer and started to provoke Pearce by swearing at him. He had been cooking eggs for their meal, but his woman refused to eat hers. By this time Pearce was fed up with her truculent behaviour and threatened to throw the egg in her face if she did not eat it. Her response was to kick him and he struck back. A furious struggle ensued during which both parties hit each other with any household items that came to hand; Pearce received a blow from a kettle of hot water, but then struck out at the woman so severely that she died from her injuries. Pearce was punished with a mere eight months in prison on account of the fight having been started by the other party, though there was only his own evidence to support this.

Rows between lovers frequently ended in the courtroom. A case with similarities to that of William Pearce took place at the 'Horse & Jockey' pub in Dover in 1844. An Irish brush salesman named Cockering was staying there with his lover, Julia McCarthy. One day the landlord was alerted by sounds of a furious struggle upstairs and dashed to their room to find that Cockering had beaten the woman senseless with a hedge-stake. The landlord ordered Cockering to run for a doctor, but the Irishman sulkily refused and the poor woman soon died. Cockering was tried for manslaughter in July 1844 but the charge was amended to one of common assault for which he received a minor punishment.

Drink also played a part in the manslaughter of Richard Cox at the 'Windmill' public house at Throwley near Faversham in 1847. A large crowd had assembled in the district in connection with a ploughing match arranged by the Faversham Agricultural Society and, as was customary, many adjourned to the pub afterwards. One of the drinkers was Edward Spillett, clearly an argumentative character. Spillett soon got involved in a row which was settled in his favour by the use of fists. Soon afterwards he got into another disagreement, this time with Richard Cox. Again it was decided to sort the matter out with the fists, but in the fight Cox soon began to show his superiority over the tiring Spillett. Spillett's response was to take out a knife and stab Cox in the stomach; the wounded man was observed to suddenly stand up and cry out, 'I'm a stabbed man, he's done me'. Then he collapsed to the ground with his entrails protruding. Spillett ran off but was arrested at his home later that day, where he was calmly eating his supper and using the same knife with which he had killed Cox. He was found guilty of manslaughter and transported for fifteen years.

It would appear that drink and passion were the two main causes of manslaughter, an especially deadly mixture when combined. Throughout the Victorian years there were cases similar to those described above, though often the distinction between murder and manslaughter became very slight.

2 The Deaf Man of Westerham, 1874

Even the saddest of trials were occasionally lightened by some touch of humour or farce and this was so in the trial of John Chatfield of Westerham for manslaughter. Chatfield was extremely deaf and throughout his trial had to be spoken to through a speaking tube inserted into his ear.

Chatfield and his wife came from the lower orders of society and were well-known around Westerham for their bad tempers and heavy drinking. The offence for which Chatfield was tried was the manslaughter of his wife, which occurred on the highway near Riverhead. It appeared from the evidence of other travellers on the road in 1874 that the Chatfields were attempting to walk home whilst in a state of considerable intoxication. Mrs Chatfield was so drunk that she could only manage a few steps before falling down, whereupon her husband had to drag her back onto her feet – only for the process to be repeated a few yards later. Each time Chatfield's wife fell down he kicked her severely, taking out some of the anger he felt on account of having lost their lodgings because of her drunkenness. Several passers-by observed him kicking her and the stupefied woman actually complained to one traveller that 'He's murdering me by inches'. This statement proved to be virtually correct, for the severe kicking she had received from her husband caused internal bleeding from which the unfortunate woman died. Despite being elderly, Chatfield was confined to prison for her manslaughter.

3 The Captain of the *Mangerton*, 1856

Manslaughter did not just apply to men or women who killed someone with their bare hands, but was also applied to careless railwaymen who caused accidents or to captains of ships whose dereliction of duty resulted in drownings. There were several examples of railwaymen in Victorian Kent being tried for manslaughter, of which one of the most typical was a result of an accident at Sittingbourne station in August 1878. On this occasion some wagons had been carelessly shunted across the path of a Ramsgate to London passenger train and in the ensuing collision five people were killed. The accident was considered to be entirely due to the carelessness of the goods yard foreman and he was tried for manslaughter, receiving a sentence of three years in prison.

On 2nd February 1856 the *Josephine Willis* set sail from St Katherine's Dock in London, with sixty-five emigrants and a crew of forty aboard. The next day, a Sunday, was clear and the *Josephine Willis* proceeded into the Channel at a steady seven knots. Later that night the ship was in collision with a steamer named the *Mangerton*, as a result of which some seventy people aboard the *Josephine Willis* were drowned as their ship sank quickly. An investigation was immediately ordered and the captain of the *Mangerton*, George Boucher, was charged with manslaughter.

Much of the evidence against Boucher was concerned with the direction and course of the *Mangerton*. It was alleged that the steamer suddenly changed course and bore down upon the *Josephine Willis* unexpectedly. One of the emigrant ship's crew saved himself by leaping across from his own ship to the *Mangerton* at the moment of collision and reported that he could not see any officer on duty or any lookout watching for other vessels. Boucher and the mate were in fact down in the cabin at the moment of impact, examining charts. The wheel of the *Mangerton* was in the charge of an illiterate boatswain. Discussion centred upon whether Boucher had been neglecting his duties by being in the cabin and whether the *Mangerton* had been displaying the correct lights. Boucher was indeed fortunate, for the court decided that he was not to blame for the accident and he was duly freed – but it had been a close call, with a fair amount of evidence suggesting that he had not been entirely efficient in the discharge of his responsibilities.

4 The Vicar who Poisoned a Parishioner

In the more rural parts of the County of Kent there tended to be few educated men in a village apart from the parson and the squire. Doctors were few and far between. Reverend Timins of West Malling had been a country parson in West Malling for over forty years when he ran into severe trouble as a result of having tried to help his parishioners; in 1883 he was charged with the manslaughter of sixteen-year-old Sarah Wright.

Rev. Timins had made use of his own education by contributing to the physical as well as the spiritual health of the parishioners. He had become a sort of amateur doctor, travelling into nearby towns to collect medicines and then treating the villagers whenever they needed assistance. However, Timins was always something of a quack and though well-known to local chemists who tried to advise him he had no expert knowledge. On 14th December 1882 Timins visited the home of the Wright family where teenage Sarah was ill. He examined her for a while and decided to administer a small dose of medicinal arsenic. He instructed the girl to take the medicine with a glass of water, but despite his protests she refused to drink the water. A short while later the girl started to foam at the mouth, vomited profusely and collapsed; she was soon dead.

The girl's family knew that Sarah had been given 'something from a bottle' by the Vicar and within a short while he was arrested and sensationally charged with manslaughter. At his trial Timins was clearly in some danger due to being a mere 'quack' as far as medicine was concerned, but several local chemists appeared to testify to his having received careful instruction about how to administer 'oil of bitter almonds'. Timins had been told that the medicine must be taken with water and produced witnesses to say that he had also told Sarah this. As the trial proceeded it became evident that the girl's refusal to drink water had distressed the Vicar at the time and led to her own death, so a highly-relieved Timins was duly discharged completely free of guilt.

CHAPTER THREE

FOOTPADS, THIEVES & SHEEP-RUSTLERS

The majority of thefts in Victorian Kent were extremely minor involving only small sums of money or quantities of food. Most of the criminals in these cases came from poor backgrounds or were children in the early teenage years. There was a direct connection between poverty and theft for, in an age when the only means of 'social security' was the workhouse, many people were forced into stealing food or money to feed their families; in the workhouse parents were separated from their children and husbands from their wives, so even to the normally honest person crime was preferable. Particularly in the earlier part of the Victorian Age, Kent was a largely rural County with an agricultural economy: a result of this was seasonal unemployment so that this type of minor crime tended to be seasonal as well. Some types of theft, like sheep-stealing, were almost entirely concerned with obtaining food for a starving family. Nonetheless, there were also a number of professional thieves who were often very well organised indeed and who eluded the authorities for years at a time.

1 The Swell Mob

Kellow Chesney's excellent book *The Victorian Underworld* tells us a great deal about a particular type of criminal gang called the 'Swell Mob'. These were groups of highly organised and skilful thieves who formed the elite of the criminal world, their skills enabling them to build up a highly comfortable lifestyle whilst their careful planning helped them to avoid arrest. The 'Swell Mob' was not one gang but a general term applied to these smart practitioners of crime, though for the Kent journalist the term was used to describe virtually any criminal from London.

Once the railways opened the Swell Mob paid frequent visits to Kent, plying their skills as pickpockets. They were attracted by any occasion when large crowds were gathered together, since it was much safer to pick pockets in the middle of a jostling mass where people were constantly bumping into each other. Particularly popular were markets and race meetings when large amounts of cash were being carried around, and even public executions provided considerable opportunity. The Swell Mob always dressed up for these occasions, since a wealthy appearance was always a protection against accusation whilst a person conspicuously from the 'lower orders' tended to attract suspicious glances.

The Maidstone Cattle Fair was a favourite haunt of the Swell Mob since it was certain that a number of wealthy and inebriated farmers would be there. An incident at the Cattle Fair in the autumn of 1837 highlighted the methods of the Swell Mob, in this case working as a gang of two young men and an older one. Unlike less professional criminals who tended to rely on sudden opportunity, the

Swell Mob carefully staked out a target before going into action. On this occasion they patrolled Maidstone High Street, 'sounding' the crowd; this was a process whereby the gang mingled with the jostling crowd, feeling for a pocket containing a bulging wallet. The gang on this occasion were not clever enough and were spotted doing the 'sounding' by an alert policeman who chased them off. However, they had had time to identify a profitable target and moved on to the next stage of the operation – creating a diversion. Whilst the two younger criminals positioned themselves close to the wealthy farmer they had selected, the older man pretended to lose control of his horse and let it run into the crowd – causing much bumping and shoving during which the farmer's pocket was successfully picked. The gang would have got away with £15 except for the alert policeman who caught up with them and managed an arrest. However the gang was not sent to prison due to a legal technicality that arose at their trial.

Tunbridge Wells also attracted the Swell Mob because of its affluent clientele. However, the mob did not always pick pockets, but sometimes took advantage of their respectable dress to deceive and trick shopkeepers. In 1847 a couple of well-dressed young criminals succeeded in swindling a Tunbridge Wells shopkeeper out of £70 worth of cloth, a sizeable haul. In fact their success was so large that it was self-defeating, for the Swell Mob were faced with the problem of how to get the cloth back to London where they could sell it. There was too much of it to carry as ordinary luggage, so they decided to bundle it into a hamper and send it by the normal railway parcels service. It did not take the Police long to identify a suspicious hamper waiting at Tunbridge Wells station as containing the stolen material and on this occasion the Constabulary proved to be smarter than the Swell Mob. The hamper was allowed to continue its journey to London Bridge, from where it was taken to an address in Newington with the police following at a discreet distance. They subsequently raided the house, which was inhabited by a group of young men and women, to find that it contained a large hoard of stolen property with origins in Kent and London.

2 Highway Robbery

By the late 1830s the 'highwayman' as such was a thing of the past, but there was still a great deal of crime on the roads of Kent. Attacks on stagecoaches or travellers on horseback were rare, but those who travelled by foot were still an easy target for the 'footpads' who were the muggers of their day. Remote country lanes at night posed plentiful opportunities for these often vicious criminals, but before gas-lighting was fully introduced even the streets of major towns could be dangerous at night.

Footpads often worked in twos or threes so that one could disable the victim whilst the other robbed him or her. This was demonstrated in an attack on a pedestrian at Chatham Hill in September 1837, when the victim was immobilised by having a sack put over his head.

A type of highway thief common in London was the 'dragsman'. This type of criminal used to loiter by the roadside and, whenever a heavily laden cart passed by, would dart out to snatch cases or bags from off it whilst the driver was not looking. Luggage was often tied onto carts, so the dragsman had to use a knife to cut it free. A dragsman was at work between Rainham and Sittingbourne in 1837, one of his successes being to 'liberate' two cases of clothes from the back of a passing chaise. Outside of London it was often difficult to dispose of stolen goods and on this occasion the dragsman fell foul of the authorities when he raised the suspicions of a pawnbroker in Chatham. The pawnbroker had decided that there was something rather unusual about a man trying to get rid of five waistcoats all at once and called in the authorities.

A young and attractive woman was a useful member of any street or highway robbers' gang. The woman could often be used to distract the victim's attention, or even as an excuse to start an argument. In July 1837 Corporal Charles Ball was stopped by a woman in Military Road, Chatham; given the nature of this district of Chatham at the time, the Corporal probably assumed that she was a prostitute. Just after he had started talking to her in an amorous manner, a man came along who claimed to be her husband, said that Ball had insulted his wife, and knocked the soldier to the ground. When Ball recovered from the blow he found that his watch had been stolen. The thief was caught through the help of a local pawnbroker but, despite all the evidence against him, was found 'not guilty'.

The combination of alcohol and the temptations of a pretty woman caused trouble for numerous soldiers, who were ruthlessly 'set up' by local footpads and their girlfriends. Marine Newman was drinking heavily in a public house in Maidstone in June 1838 when he attracted the attentions of a young woman, showing off by buying drinks for everyone. Newman and the young woman started to walk back to Chatham together that night, but what he had presumably hoped to be a romantic opportunity turned out to be a painful experience! Once away from Maidstone, Newman was waylaid by two men who knocked him down, jumped on him and rifled his pockets before escaping into the dark with the young woman. The two men were later caught and one of them admitted that the girl was his wife; the leader of the group, Richardson, was transported for life.

Footpads tended to 'work' particular areas for a while and then move on. Thus the road between Loose and Maidstone was a dangerous place for a while in 1838 and in 1840 a group of armed footpads terrorised the Sittingbourne area. The latter group were notably ambitious, actually attacking a coach and also breaking into a house at Tunstall, where they were scared off by the butler who fired a shotgun through a window they had opened.

Another young man who learnt to be more careful with women was a farmer who visited Canterbury in March 1844. He received the keen attentions of a young woman, but once out in the street with her he was 'collared by a powerful fellow' and roughed up. In the course of the struggle the farmer was relieved of £6.

Another gang of footpads infested the Faversham area in 1844-1845. In January of the latter year a Mr Shepherd of Faversham, who was a pipe-maker, was attacked by three men between Boughton and Canterbury. This gang operated in the usual organised footpad manner – one pinioned his arms, one stopped his mouth, and the other rifled his pockets and took 9s.6d. A similar gang, this time of five, operated in the triangle bordered by Maidstone, Tenterden and Ashford in 1847, working mostly on the evenings after a market day when they could prey on farmers returning home with cash in their pockets. The gang was based in Canterbury but used the trains so they could operate outside their home area; they were not careful enough and two of them, Piety and Haisman, were eventually caught at the station in Canterbury. At their trial it was reported that they knocked their victims down and pulled their trousers round their knees so they could not run away. They were sentenced to ten and fourteen years' transportation respectively.

The footpad was a dying breed, however, and by the 1870s attacks on the open road were far less frequent. Fewer farmers carried their cash with them, and the wealthiest travellers went by train or carriage. The footpad continued to be a menace only in the larger towns like Chatham, where they preyed on the drunken and the foolish.

3 Sheep-Stealing

Thefts of animals in Victorian Kent were quite rare with the single exception of sheep. Even then the offence was fairly small scale, there being few occasions when more than one or two animals were taken. The reason for this was that most animals were stolen for food rather than money and the sheep was the ideal size. It could be caught and killed easily, then rapidly skinned in the middle of a field under cover of darkness. The first the farmer was likely to know about the crime was when he arrived at his field the next morning to find a bloody skin where there had previously been a healthy animal. 'Rustling' as such was virtually non-existent because it was very difficult to escape detection when trailing thirty or forty sheep around the countryside.

Amongst the various types of thefts, the stealing of sheep was always the most severely punished; indeed, in the earlier part of the Victorian period it was invariably punished with transportation. This was because it struck most directly at the ruling-class of the County, the farmers and landowners whose greatest belief was in the sanctity and inviolability of landed property. The theft of animals, which included poaching, was therefore seen as an attack on the established order of society and – even if prompted by starvation – was not to be tolerated.

An example of a man who stole a sheep to feed his family was Thomas Drew of East Peckham. His case exhibited several classic features of the genre, the first being that it occurred in the depths of the winter of 1837-8; winter was always a difficult time when employment prospects were at their lowest. Drew stole one sheep from a nearby field, later claiming that he did so in order to feed his daughters. When the farmer became aware of his loss, Drew was an immediate suspect and a policeman visited his house. The unfortunate man had attempted to avoid detection by cutting the meat up into small pieces and hiding it in various nooks and crannies around his home, but the policeman uncovered evidence easily enough. Pieces of mutton were found in the wash-house, under the stone floor near Drew's oven, and even in a coat pocket upstairs. Drew was arrested, convicted for theft, and transported to Australia for fifteen years; his daughters were presumably taken to the workhouse.

Two years later a rather more enterprising pair of sheep-stealers were caught in an amphibious operation off the coast near Allhallows. The two thieves were part of the crew of a ship which had been sailing up the River Thames and, in passing the marshes at Allhallows in January 1840, their attention had been attracted to a number of sheep grazing there unattended. The two mariners quickly decided that it would be an easy matter to row the ship's boat in to the shore, kill and skin a sheep, then row back to the ship with the meat. They had not reckoned on the alert coastguards in the area, however, for these authorities noticed the curious behaviour of the ship and were able to arrest the two criminals with the sheep actually in their rowing boat.

This scale of operation was normal for the sheep-stealer and larger scale affairs were rare. One of those rare crimes occurred at Bradbourne, near Sevenoaks, in 1845. Edward Boswell had at one time been a butcher in Sevenoaks, but in February 1845 he turned to crime by stealing forty-nine sheep from a field at Bradbourne. The farmer, as usual, discovered his loss the next morning; he did not need much imagination to guess what had happened to his flock, since the field was close to the London to Sevenoaks turnpike road.

Boswell's plan was to drive the sheep to London where he could sell them to a butcher. However he had decided that the turnpike road was not a safe route to travel and so opted for a roundabout course which he hoped would throw the inevitable pursuers off his trail. There had been a light fall of snow, however, and this enabled the authorities to follow the tracks of the sheep. Boswell's route was indeed circuitous, for it wound through Riverhead, Chipstead, Knockholt and Cudham to Leaves Green on the Westerham to London road. There the trail vanished, for there had not been any snow in that part of Kent and frost had left the ground so hard that there were no traces of the sheep.

Boswell might have got away with his daring and unusual crime, had he not begun to lose his nerve on the approach to London. Whilst the authorities were still scouring the Westerham area, he had been heading for Croydon and he eventually arrived at the Surrey village of Beddington. Perhaps the large flock was proving too much for him, or perhaps he felt a smaller flock would be less suspicious, but in Beddington he attempted to sell half the sheep for slaughter to a local butcher. This would have been an unusual thing for a normal shepherd to have done and the butcher had his doubts about Boswell; he skilfully kept him engaged in conversation whilst sending a message to the local constable, as a result of which Boswell was questioned and his crime discovered. A daring crime had failed through a last minute loss of nerve.

Horses were less rarely stolen, largely because they were more easily traced. Two Strood boys, of nine and eleven years old, stole a horse for a lark in 1894 and rode it all the way to Northfleet where they abandoned it. Fifty years earlier they might have received a very severe punishment for such a crime, but in 1894 the penalty was six strokes of the birch each.

4 Thieves at Large!

The majority of thefts in Victorian Kent were minor and trivial just as they are today, but in the 1800s they often carried very heavy penalties. The West Kent Quarter Sessions of July 1837 showed that people were taken to court for the most petty of crimes, for they were judged to have committed a serious offence by violating the taboo of property-rights. On that particular occasion, individuals were prosecuted for the theft of a plank and also of a whip from a cart; in the latter case the punishment was three months hard labour. Labour was the usual penalty for theft, but if someone's house had been entered illegally the punishment was more severe; a Chatham burglar of 1837 was transported for life.

The theft of clothing was a common practice, though the problem with this was finding a way of disposing of the excess apparel for profit. In a big city like London it was no problem at all, but in Kent it was much harder to find a reliable 'fence'. William Francis, a nineteen-year-old youth from Sittingbourne had this problem when he stole five pairs of trousers; he realised that the Sittingbourne pawnbrokers would know him and so he went to Chatham to dispose of his goods. In Chatham he went to a pawnbroker named Levi who was instantly suspicious; very few working men owned two pairs of trousers, so anyone with five pairs to dispose of was almost bound to be dishonest! Francis was duly arrested.

Burglary was regarded as more serious than theft. John Morris received a sentence of ten years' transportation in 1838 even though he had only attempted to steal one handkerchief, a jacket and a pair of trousers. His real crime was that he had broken into a house in Wrotham to obtain them where he was, incidentally, caught in the act. Burglary from the homes of the wealthy was always risky since servants were always on duty and any sound might alert them.

A more sophisticated type of thief was the forger, commonly known as a 'smasher'. Forgers usually took advantage of the multiplicity of banks that existed at a time when most towns of any size had their own banking company. Forged cheques were a common problem, which was the method used by Nathaniel Isaacs of Chatham in 1839. Isaacs had got into debt of £2,000 and tried to wriggle his way out of the situation by forging cheques. He persuaded various people, including several army officers, to accept these cheques in exchange for cash; he managed to raise some £10,000 in this way, a quite considerable sum. It was unwise for a forger to operate too much in one area, so Isaacs took off for Gravesend where he swindled the London & County Bank out of yet more cash. However, he had perhaps over-reached himself and the authorities were alerted. He fled to Dover where, with the authorities closing in, he locked himself in a room at the 'Victoria Hotel' and took poison.

Banks were much more prone to losing their money to forgers than they were to more traditional bank-robbers. A rare bank raid occurred in Maidstone in 1841, when the Kentish Bank was relieved of £500 in gold.

Another subtle form of theft was embezzlement. Railway booking office clerks were always prone to run off with the takings, as were shop assistants; in fact this sort of crime was so common as to arouse little public interest. Altogether more sensational was the arrest of Rochester's Superintendent of Police for embezzlement in 1842. His name was Cork and one of his duties had been to arrange the collection and safe-keeping of the Borough Rates. Sadly not all the money found its way into the correct bank account, since Cork siphoned off £70 for himself. At his trial he attempted to argue his way out of transportation by pleading that his wife and eleven children would starve without him, but he was not successful.

It is interesting to examine one minor crime in more detail and to look at a type of theft that has now vanished altogether. In June 1843 the 'Swan Inn' at Malling shut its doors at about ten o'clock, the gates leading into the yard and stables being securely fastened for the night. When the staff got up at six o'clock the next morning it was found that someone had climbed over the gates, broken into the carriage-shed and destroyed the seating inside three or four coaches. The seats had been ripped apart and all the horsehair stuffing removed; it was, everyone said, a repeat of a crime that had taken place in Wrotham a few days earlier.

The staff of the 'Swan Inn' reckoned that the criminal was still in the neighbourhood so a hue and cry was set up, but no-one was found. The following day a tramp paid a visit to a saddler's shop in Dartford and offered a quantity of horsehair for sale. The sadler was suspicious, for tramps did not turn up with 37lbs of horsehair every day and questioned the man – George Smith – very carefully. Smith declared that he had ripped the horsehair out of some old matresses, but the sadler was alerted by its quality. A policeman was sent for and Smith was arrested when a piece of carriage lining was found in the horsehair. This material was found to match the carriages damaged at Wrotham but not at Malling, though it was soon found out that Smith was part of a gang that had been involved with both crimes. The horsehair from the 'Swan Inn' had already been sold for 18s.6d., though to get it the tramps had destroyed over £30 worth of carriage seating. Smith was sent to prison, but his friends were never captured.

There was a great deal of minor theft during the 1840s when the economic position was very poor and potato blight had worsened the situation. Again food was a main target, though the occasional criminal managed to add a touch of humour to the proceedings. One man killed and skinned a sheep in a field near Sarre, leaving behind the skin and a message for the distraught farmer. It read:

'Potatoes are scarce and turnips are thin
I've got your mutton – you may have the skin.'

At a time when there were no pensions for the elderly, several old people turned to stealing in order to avoid the workhouse. Poor old George Benge of

The Gravesend Potato Thief

Gravesend had fallen on hard times by 1866 and was feeling very hungry on the day he broke into someone's garden and stole one potato; he was caught and sentenced to twenty-eight days' hard labour. Sometimes the legal system was very heartless.

Two professional burglars operated throughout Kent in 1881-1882, named Hart and Glover. Their speciality was railway stations, where they had developed a technique of forcing their way into booking offices at night and stealing the day's takings. In their extensive career they successfully raided the railway stations at Sittingbourne, Herne Bay, Walmer, Canterbury, Sandwich, Sturry and Whitstable before they were finally caught and sent to prison.

Pubs tended to be centres of crime, but it was not often that a publican was actually the victim of a crime. In 1895 a man entered a public house in Rochester and attempted to make off with a silver cruet. The publican spotted him, attempted to grapple with the thief and a fight ensued in which the publican's ear was bitten off. It took four Police constables to subdue the thief and when he appeared in the dock at the Magistrates' Court he was still fighting furiously. This Court must have been a strange occasion, since the publican's ear – pickled in a jar of spirits – was produced as evidence. The fighting thief was sent for trial at the Quarter Sessions, where he received his just punishment in the shape of three years of penal servitude.

CHAPTER FOUR

SEX AND THE FAMILY, A CATALOGUE OF CRIMES OF PASSION

The Victorian outlook on marriage was a peculiar mixture of diverse opinions and practices. Amidst the working class, 'marriage' was often hard to define since it rarely had any legal significance; couples tended to live together and, after a while, were generally accepted as 'man and wife'. The ties were therefore fairly soluble and in isolated rural communities a certain amount of husband- or wife-swapping was far from unusual; it has already been noted that the complicated emotional strains that resulted often ended in violent disagreement and occasionally death.

For the middle-class marriage often tended to be a matter of making a good match and the social position of one's partner was an important factor. Middle-class men in the Victorian age tended to get married much later than is the case in the 1980s, the prevalent view being that a wife should be 'provided for' in the style to which she was accustomed; therefore a man tended to delay marriage until he had built up a useful income. In London this was seen by some commentators as a cause of the prevalence of prostitution, but in the smaller towns of Kent it would have been unwise for a middle-class man to frequent any house of ill-repute for the gossip would soon spread. Prostitution in Kent tended to be directly related to the presence of soldiers in a town.

These different attitudes towards marriage resulted in types of 'crime' being common in Victorian Kent that are now rare or, in one case, have disappeared altogether.

1 Wedding Vows

Bigamy was a fairly common crime in which it was usually a male who was at fault. It was easy for a man to have more than one wife at a time when state records could not easily be compared and when it was relatively easy for a man to travel around the country, assuming a different name in each town he came to. Bigamy was a crime particularly favoured by soldiers and seamen, who might find it the only way to overcome a girl's resistance to seduction before moving on to their next base. The case of Samuel Jeston in 1837 was therefore very unusual; Jeston was a mulatto surgeon from Rochester who in the course of his travels had picked up an extra wife. It was an unusual event for a man of his profession to be accused of bigamy and, when found guilty, he was punished severely with seven years' transportation.

During the earlier part of the Victorian age a man could be prosecuted for deserting his wife and family. This was not because of any state sympathy for the position of the unlucky wife, indeed before the Married Women's Property Act (1870) a husband could do whatever he liked with his wife's property. The authorities were likely to be interested in the case of a deserting husband only if he left his wife and children without any means of support, a situation which would mean they would become a further burden to the workhouse. In 1886 another Act, the Maintenance of Wives (Desertion) Act, at last stipulated that if a man ran off he could be made to pay £2 a week to his deserted wife; before this date the authorities only cared when they had to foot the bill.

One man who incurred the wrath of the Kent authorities was Samuel Bone of Maidstone, who deserted his wife and children in 1837. As was usually the case, the man ran off because he had found a new woman – Bone had fallen in love with the widow of his old employer. The widow obviously had some spare cash, for the two eloped with ease and were only tracked down with some difficulty to Surrey. As the *Maidstone Journal* reported, Bone was 'recently discovered . . . keeping a beer-shop in Surrey with his paramour'. His punishment for forcing the Borough of Maidstone to feed and clothe his family was one month's hard labour.

At the start of the Victorian era there were occasional prosecutions for 'Breach of Promise', but their number declined steadily towards the end of the century; this was probably due to the unwelcome glare of publicity that they brought to what was often a sad case. It took a really vindictive parent to expose his daughter to such public discussion.

One young lady who was left chastened by her experiences with a lover whose ardour cooled was Miss Julia Neame of Margate. Miss Neame was the daughter of a wealthy man who lived at the Kent resort, but she must have been lacking in some of the qualities necessary to make a good 'match', since at the age of twenty-six she was still unmarried and filling up her time by teaching at a ladies' college in the town. This would suggest that she either lacked the traditional feminine beauties or was at the end of a large family, because of which any marriage 'settlement' might have been small.

In 1840 Miss Neame met a Mr Ellis, who was making a visit to Margate from his home at Greenhithe. Ellis began paying close attention to Miss Neame, which the young lady encouraged, and in due course a proposal of marriage was made and accepted. The great emphasis placed by the Victorian middle-class on social position and money in marriage in fact opened that class up to a certain type of confidence trickster – a man with all the social graces, but no real property, who could engineer a profitable marriage for himself. It may have been that Ellis was just that sort of predator, for his devotion to Miss Neame can only have been wafer-thin. For, having gone back to Greenhithe, he soon wrote to Miss Neame's father to say that he wished to be released from his proposal of marriage.

The grounds that Ellis gave were, on the surface, reasonable enough since they were common amongst the Victorian middle-class – he said that his own father disapproved of the match. But Ellis was lying, for on his return to Greenhithe he had met a young woman of independent fortune named Miss Watkins; obviously a smooth-talking charmer, Ellis had wormed his way into her heart and they had been married within a few months. Therefore his real reason for wanting to cancel his marriage to Miss Neame was that he was already married!

Mr Neame soon found out the awful truth and prosecuted Ellis for 'Breach of Promise'. It was quite clear to the court that Ellis had acted in a most deceitful and dishonourable manner, motivated solely by the desire for personal profit. He was found guilty and fined £400, a quite considerable sum.

One man who did not quite make it to the wedding vows was Patrick Curran, who had planned to get married in Canterbury during 1847. Curran's fiancée lived out in the country and had to travel some distance to Canterbury, so he did not see her for several days before the wedding. On the day itself he awaited her arrival, but neither she nor her family showed up. Curran concluded that he had been 'stood up' and spent the rest of the day in a bout of heavy drinking. During his binge he got talking with a young woman named Amelia Carey, one of a family of notorious daughters. Curran did not intend spending what was meant to be his 'wedding night' alone and he took Amelia back to his room. When he woke the next morning he found that the girl had left, taking with her his watch and his money. She was soon arrested and all his property was found in her possession. At this point Curran's bride and her family turned up, having been delayed on their journey, to find the erstwhile 'groom' in a position of some shame and disgrace. The local press did not record whether the couple actually got married or not.

Most bigamists were men, so the case of a female bigamist at Dover in 1866 attracted great interest. Jane Forge turned the table on the normally unreliable soldiers by trying to beat them at their own game! On 18th March 1862 she married John Forge, a soldier. Within a few weeks her new husband left for India but Jane found consolation in another man's arms for she moved to Dover and there married Almond Newman, who was also a soldier. Newman was also posted abroad and pleaded for Jane to go with him, but she refused. At her trial she defended herself by claiming that she had believed Forge to be dead, but evidence was produced to show that she had continued to claim Forge's pay all the time he was away in India – a sum of about £90. Eventually Forge returned and he and Jane resumed their life together until the truth came out and Jane was brought to court; Forge had obviously forgiven her, though, since they continued to live together during the trial. Jane Forge was punished with one week in prison.

Few working-class families could afford to occupy a house by themselves and so 'the lodger' was a common feature of Victorian life. Unfortunately the presence of another male in the house tended to be too much of a temptation for some women and there were numerous cases of a wife running off with the lodger and leaving a grieving husband. This was not against the law in itself, but absconding wives tended to take some of the household possessions with them and could therefore be prosecuted for theft. John Clark of Otford was one man who had such an experience. At the start of 1866 he was sent to gaol for a month and during this time his wife became very intimate with their lodger, sleeping with him in the couple's feather bed. When Clark was released from prison he went home to find his wife missing, his lodger missing and his feather bed missing as well! The lodger, thirty-two year old Thomas Watson, was soon arrested and charged with the theft of the bed, for which he received six months' hard labour.

Occasionally domestic rows involving lodgers became so complicated that even the courts despaired of working out what had actually happened. One case like this involved Benjamin Dangerfield of Luton, near Chatham, who in 1894 was charged with deserting his wife. Dangerfield's defence was that she was a shrewish, 'bitter woman' and he had left her because she was having an affair with his lodger. There then unfolded a most ridiculous story of domestic disharmony and suspicion. It turned out that the Dangerfields had fallen on hard times and that the wife, Lottie, had pawned the family blankets in the middle of the winter. Only the lodger had any blankets and the fact that he had the advantage over his landlord and landlady clearly caused some arguing between them since the blankets he used belonged to them. A compromise was eventually reached, whereby all three lay down to sleep in front of the fire. Dangerfield claimed that this intimacy sparked off some feeling between his wife and the lodger; he claimed that they 'embraced' during the night, by which he clearly meant something more passionate than mere kissing. Dangerfield also claimed that on occasions he had left the house when his wife and the lodger were there and almost immediately the blinds had been drawn; what were they doing that called for secrecy?

Lottie put up a spirited defence of her honour, denying that anything had been going on with the lodger. Instead she claimed that the lodger had been cruel to her and had driven two hair pins into her head. Eventually the court adjourned in despair and no more came of the case.

It was not only lodgers that caused jealousy but also neighbours. Another Chatham case of 1894 involved John Allen of Jerusalem Row. Allen had developed a suspicion about the behaviour of a neighbour, William Hills, who he thought had been luring his wife into his house, plying her with drink and then taking advantage of her. Evidence given about Allen's wife suggested that she was a heavy drinker in any case, but there was little to suggest that there was any truth in his suspicion of a romantic liaison. But Allen harboured a grudge for several weeks until, one day, it all became too much for him and he decided to seek vengeance. He burst into Hills' house like a furious whirlwind, scattering furniture everywhere. Allen threw a basket of shrimps at the unfortunate and cowering Hills, following it up with a plate, two tables and a few punches. Hills and his wife fled out into the street, but Allen followed them and attacked them with a poker before others helped to restrain the furious man. Allen was tried for assault and during the course of the trial it emerged that there was no truth whatever in his suspicions; he was sentenced to six weeks' hard labour.

Towards the end of the century the authorities became much more concerned with the duties of parents with respect to their children. This was largely due to the National Society for the Prevention of Cruelty to Children, which in several highly-publicised cases prosecuted parents for the neglect of their children and

The Attack by John Allen on his neighbours

thereby galvanized the authorities into some sort of action. A number of cases of cruelty to children or neglect emerged in the mid-1890s. In October 1894 Frederick Essex accused the porter at the Medway Union Workhouse of trying to seduce his daughter, who was under sixteen years old; at the trial the girl sensationally announced that it was not the porter who was at fault but her own father, who was trying to force her to become an 'unfortunate' or prostitute for his own financial gain. The following year Eliza Green was prosecuted for 'exposing her children', which was a result of having taken out her four children – including a babe in arms – on a begging expedition in the middle of winter. Like Essex, Green also hoped to profit from her children since the sight of starving little children helped to tug at the consciences of passers-by and therefore improved the profitability of begging. Eliza Green was given four months' hard labour.

Pure malice was evident in the case of a Bearsted man the same year, who kept his eight-year-old boy on a diet of bread and water for weeks at a time. The child was also regularly thrashed with a stick and in the end ran off into the snow, where he nearly died of frostbite. The wicked parent was given some hard labour so that he could experience some suffering for himself.

At about the same time, in Chatham, a mother was arrested after four-year-old Joseph Lodge starved to death. This was a case which had involved the NSPCC and, like all their work, it had been carefully documented. The Magistrates heard that Mrs Lodge was a widow with five children, who lived in a two-roomed house. Joseph appears to have died because he had not been properly fed for a very long time, rather than because his mother had deliberately starved him. A doctor reported that the child's body was emaciated and covered with flea bites. At the age of four years and eight months he weighed only twenty-six pounds, whereas the average child at that age weighed thirty-six pounds. The NSPCC inspector reported that the house and beds were full of fleas and that it was a case of long-term neglect. Mrs Lodge was committed for trial at the Assizes, but it was obvious that the real moral fault lay with the Victorian social philosophy that offered only the workhouse – and therefore the loss of her children – to a mother who could not cope financially.

Breach of Promise cases had become very rare by the end of the century, but such a case was successfully brought in 1895. Miss Eva Froude was a butcher's daughter from Hunton near Maidstone who went into domestic service with a wealthy London costumier named Snell. In due course Eva attracted the attention of Snell's son, Dr Sidney Snell, who lived at Grays in Essex. An engagement was contracted, but before the couple could get married Dr Snell suddenly broke it off. Eva Froude's father sued for Breach of Promise, arguing that Dr Snell had deserted his daughter because of the difference in their social class; it would certainly have been fairly unusual for a member of a middle-class profession to have married one of his father's domestic servants.

Dr Snell defended his position by arguing that the girl had misled him. He argued that they had become engaged on the understanding that there was no consumption (or tuberculosis) in Miss Froude's family, since the doctor believed that this was a hereditary disease and did not want to have children with it. Eva had assured him that there was not, but Dr Snell had subsequently discovered that her mother had died of consumption and thus broke off the engagement. The jury was not taken in by this deception and found in favour of Miss Froude, with very heavy damages of £1,000.

2 Indecency

The word 'indecency' was often used by cautious Victorian journalists to draw a veil across the details of numerous types of crime. In those days, the press was rather more delicate in what it actually said, though it was just as lurid in what it hinted at. There were one or two Victorian crimes of indecency which are no longer heard of, such as the charge of committing an 'unnatural offence with an animal' which was levelled against a youth from Hoo; he was acquitted, presumably because the animal could not give evidence. A number of charges of indecent behaviour were directed against prostitutes as detailed later, one of the most common being the use of profane language in the street.

Rape and indecent assault were quite common crimes and also tended to involve soldiers a great deal in the garrison towns. An unusually serious case was brought to trial in March 1842, when a total of seven young men from the small village of Hougham were transported for life as a result of an assault on a young girl in a field at three o'clock in the morning, the previous April. It was almost unknown for such a number of people to be transported for one crime, let alone for such a number from one small village.

Transportation for life was the standard punishment in the 1840s for rape or the more serious forms of indecent assault. A soldier from New Brompton was so punished in April 1843, but by the middle of the century punishments had softened somewhat. By that stage there had been a great deal of publicity about 'loose women' and courts recognised that soldiers were occasionally 'led on'; they often found it difficult to distinguish between the local flirts and the real 'gay women', and it was usually the flirts who suffered. A typical case involved Bombardier Will Flintham, who assaulted Emma Tilley in Maidstone Market during 1866. Tilley had been flirting with several soldiers in a provocative way, arousing the desires of Flintham who asked if he could 'go home with her'. When the girl refused but continued to flirt, he lost control of himself and threw her to the ground. He grabbed her by the throat and was in the act of pulling up her skirts when her screams alerted the Police. A Constable soon arrived, but was rewarded with a kick from Flintham. At his trial the soldier admitted that he had become tipsy and the girl had been teasing him. He was punished with one month's hard labour.

An unusual case of attempted indecency within a family was brought to trial in January 1874. Mrs Hull of New Brompton was a widow with a large family, who found it rather difficult to provide for her children as well as she would have liked. In 1873 the Hull children were visited by their uncle, George Fairfoot, a forty-five year old gentleman who lived in Crewe. Shortly after this visit Mrs Hull received a letter which purported to be from Fairfoot's wife offering to adopt one of her children. This was good news for Mrs Hull, who knew that the Fairfoots were quite prosperous and would be able to give a child a comfortable upbringing. On Boxing Day 1874 George Fairfoot arrived, selected fourteen-year-old Cordelia for 'adoption' and departed with her for Crewe.

Once on the train, Fairfoot told Cordelia that it was too late to journey all the way back to Crewe that night. They arrived at London Bridge station at 8pm and Fairfoot took the girl for supper at a coffee-house in Duke Street. He booked some rooms there, showed the girl into her bedroom and then left her. However the next morning Cordelia woke up to find Fairfoot in bed with her and attempting an assault. She protested strongly and he offered to buy her silk dresses and bring her up as a lady if she would let him do as he liked. The girl steadfastly refused, with the result that Fairfoot was arrested and sentenced to two years' hard labour. Earlier in the century he would almost certainly have been transported since, as a gentleman, his behaviour was considered especially shocking.

Incest was fairly commonplace at a time when families lived very close together, often with several in a bed. It was, however, rarely discovered unless a child let something slip, especially as it was more common in working-class slums or remote country villages where legal authority did not often penetrate. A rare prosecution for incest occurred in 1856. George Chapman, a bricklayer from Wrotham, was charged with assaulting and 'carnally knowing' his thirteen-year-old daughter. The girl had consented, but this was considered to be no defence since a parent could easily pressurise a child. Chapman was found guilty and transported for life.

Today we are familiar with the workings of the 'age of consent' laws, designed to protect young girls. For much of the Victorian Age this law was unknown. The landmark was really the Criminal Law Amendment Act of 1885 which set the age of consent at sixteen (it had previously been thirteen) and made it an offence for anyone to encourage a girl of under eighteen years to leave home – this was regarded as abduction. These laws were designed to suppress the great problem of child prostitution, particularly in London, but in the Counties they tended to be used more often to protect impressionable teenage girls from unscrupulous admirers. Sometimes men were not quite so 'black or white', as was the case with an eighteen-year-old Yarmouth fisherman who was arrested in Kent in 1894.

The fisherman, James Wells, was charged with having taken a fourteen-year-old girl from her father 'for an illegal purpose'. The girl and her father had been doing a fair amount of travelling around, during which they had met Wells. She had flirted with Wells and then, when she got fed up with the sort of life her father was making her lead, she eloped with him. The trial went very much in Wells' favour, for during his time with the girl he had ensured that they slept in separate rooms and several innkeepers were able to testify to this. The matter of the girl's age also came into question and it was revealed that her father had persistently misled her as to how old she really was. When it had become quite clear that Wells had done nothing indecent, the Judge dismissed the case against him.

It was not always the men who were to blame. Later the same year, three soldiers ended up in the dock at the Magistrates' Court because two Rochester girls had accused them of attacking them as they were going home one night. The two girls, aged fifteen and eighteen, alleged that the soldiers had followed them along the street at eleven o'clock one night. One of them had then grabbed the younger girl, dragged her through a hedge, and attempted to assault her. The Magistrate listened to this story very carefully then, with a few sharp questions, tore it apart. It became clear that the girls had been very late home one night and had made up the allegations in an effort to escape the wrath of their parents. One can imagine that they were even less popular with their parents after the details of the case had appeared in all the local papers!

Another case to end without prosecution of charges was the notorious Chatham 'Four in a Bed' scandal of 1895. It appeared that two teenage girls did not return to their homes on Saturday night after an evening out in the town, which then had a quite dreadful reputation for immorality. The next morning one of the anxious fathers managed to trace his daughter's movements to a house at 228 New Road, Chatham. At ten o'clock that Sunday morning, the father burst into an upstairs room at the house to find his daughter, another girl and two soldiers all in bed together.

A charge of rape was brought against the two soldiers since both girls were only fifteen years old, though it is unlikely that the soldiers knew this. It was normal for the NSPCC to take an interest in such cases, but on this occasion the NSPCC refused to have anything to do with the prosecution since, they said, the girls were both of notoriously bad character. The trials of the two soldiers revealed this, for it was a key part of the defence case. Evidence was produced to show that the two girls spent a lot of their time hanging around at the Barracks gate, accosting soldiers. They were also heavy drinkers of whisky. A key part of the defence case was the appearance of the girls, for both looked considerably older than fifteen and it was therefore argued that the soldiers could have been misled by the girls. The Defence Counsel remarked on one girl that 'He should have thought Bradley was at least eighteen, and from her utter lack of delicacy she might be fifty'. The Bradley girl was notorious for her colourful bad language! Inevitably, the two soldiers were released.

One thing that was unusual in Victorian Kent was the prosecution of a person for obscene publications, though towards the end of the era obscene photographs did start to find their way onto the market. In 1882 a man was fined £2 at Tunbridge Wells for trying to sell obscene prints to other men in a pub. His defence was that he had found the pictures in a railway carriage.

3 The 'Lewd' Vicar of Sandwich

By the 1800s the 'Church courts' of medieval times had disappeared, though it was still possible for the Church of England to 'try' one of its clergy for being in breach of accepted canons of behaviour. Thus it was that in December 1866 the Vicar of St Peter's Sandwich, Rev. H. Gilder, was charged before an Ecclesiastical Commission with 'lewdness and incontinence'.

Rev. Gilder was living at Sandwich with his wife in 1861 when he engaged Emily Taylor as a domestic servant. This girl was still fairly young and quite attractive. Mrs Gilder was evidently quite ill and, shortly after Emily had started work, she had to go away for five or six weeks to convalesce. During the time that his wife was away, Rev. Gilder found himself attracted to the new servant girl; as Emily later admitted, the result was that 'frequent intimacy took place between Mr Gilder and myself'. The Vicar plainly became quite obsessed with the girl, though he took pains to maintain the master-servant relationship between them; he even arranged for Emily to sleep in a bedroom with two doors, one of which gave onto the corridor and the other of which led directly to the Vicar's own bedroom so that he could reach her at night. This second door had a catch on the Vicar's side, so that he could gain access to her room whenever he wanted to but not vice versa. During the inquiry, the members of the Ecclesiastical Commission solemnly trooped round to the house to study this locking arrangement.

Mrs Gilder died in 1864 and Emily became very close to the Gilder children. She continued to work for Rev. Gilder for several more months, during which 'intimacy' took place in Emily's bedroom and in the dining-room. The Vicar threatened to sack the girl if she became pregnant, and this was a very real threat since pregnant servant girls were unlikely to get another job. Emily left Rev. Gilder's service in February 1865 and he gave her a good reference so that she could get another job in the town.

Rev. Gilder no longer employed Emily, but he still wished to call upon her other services and frequently invited her round to his house. The girl grew quite accustomed to his stopping her in the street and inviting her round 'to see the children'. On these occasions, Emily testified before the Commission, 'I always saw Mr Gilder in the dining-room, where he had connection with me'.

Eventually the inevitable happened and Emily became pregnant. She had to give up her job and moved to Woodnesbury, where she gave birth to a son on 21st February 1866. From the start she insisted that it was Gilder's child, as a result of which the Magistrates at Wingham served a maintenance order upon him. With that the scandal broke and the wrath of the Church came down upon the shoulders of the foolish Rev. Gilder.

The Ecclesiastical Commission decided that he had brought scandal upon the Church of England and was guilty of 'lewdness and incontinence' in his behaviour. The Justices suspended him from performing divine service and his position as Rector of St Peter's was suspended for three years. He retired from the district in shame.

4 Unwanted Babies

Contraception was not readily available in Victorian Kent, with the result that there were a large number of unwanted pregnancies. Most of these resulted in unwanted children, but there were a few backstreet abortionists who, for a fee, would cause an illegal miscarriage. One such person was Mary Sprackland of New Brompton, who was trained as a midwife but who had opted to put her skills to illegal and more profitable purposes. It was her practice to charge five shillings to supply certain 'powders', which the customer took home and administered to herself. The following morning one of Mary Sprackland's assistants would arrive at the customer's house to collect the 'evidence' which was then buried. When she was arrested in December 1895 a number of Mary Sprackland's customers turned against her, as did one of her assistants. George Dealler told the court that he thought he was helping women who had flu and did not know what was in the various small parcels that he had to collect; this was rather unlikely, since he also had to bury the parcels and could not have been that unsuspicious! An investigation of Sprackland's house centred on the contents of her cesspool, where portions of a syringe were found; this betrayed the method which she used as an alternative to 'powders'. Mary Sprackland was sent off to the Assizes for sentencing, with a heavy prison term expected.

Unwanted babies were commonly disposed of illegally by their mothers, though this was more usual with unmarried girls than with married women. The case of Mrs Hans, which occurred at Gravesend in 1845, was somewhat unusual therefore. Mrs Hans lived in New Brompton with her husband, a Private in the Army, and their baby son. Hans was posted to India and his wife was told that she could not accompany him, particularly as they had a child of only ten months old. The woman was quite distraught at the news and, when her husband left to join his ship at Gravesend, she began to plot how she could accompany him.

She decided that it was really the baby that was causing the problem and visited a Brompton pharmacist aptly named Mr Death. From him she bought some laudanum, a heavy sedative based on opium, which she gave to the baby. A large dose made the child very ill and she attempted to palm him off on the authorities at the Workhouse hospital – but they refused to accept the child. Not despairing, she took a train for Gravesend and, during the journey, the baby died.

When she got to Gravesend she put on a great show for watching people, telling them how her baby had died and engaging their sympathies. She explained that she was hurrying to meet her husband and several local people agreed to look after the child's corpse.

Mrs Hans' next step was to stow away aboard the troop ship and it was not until after the ship had left Gravesend that the true reason for the baby's death was discovered. The ship was due to call in at Portsmouth before sailing down the Channel and the authorities hoped to arrest her there, but due to a change of schedule the ship did not call in at an English port again. After part of the journey to India the stowaway was discovered, but no-one on the ship was aware of Mrs

Hans' crime. The Captain and the officers felt sorry for her, seeing her as a devoted and lovesick wife and agreed to feed her from their own supplies. The ship was well on the way to India before anyone learnt her true story and by then it was too late to turn back; Mrs Hans went all the way to India before she was arrested.

Pregnancy lay behind a charge of attempted murder in 1874. George Golds was a fairly well-to-do young man from Bromley who was clearly fairly keen on the girls. In 1873 he started 'walking out' with Eliza Baldwin from Farnborough, although he had already got himself into trouble with another girl whose child he was paying maintenance for. Nonetheless, in November 1873 Golds and Baldwin became engaged. A few months later Eliza had to tell Golds that she was pregnant, news which he did not receive too kindly; she suspected that he had another child elsewhere, but he did not actually tell her so and she supposed that his distress was due to financial worries.

In June 1874 the couple spent a few hours together in Bromley, where they had tea together including salmon sandwiches. Golds ordered a fly to take Eliza home, in which he accompanied her. On the way Eliza said that she felt ill, so they stopped the fly outside a public house and Golds went in to get her a drink. He gave her some brandy which she later said did not smell 'right', but nonetheless she drank it. When she got home she collapsed and became unconscious for a while so a doctor was called; Eliza became very ill and retched violently. The doctor suggested that she might have consumed something poisonous, as a result of which Golds was charged with having tried to kill her with the sandwiches or the brandy. During the trial Golds alleged that Eliza had taken something herself only three weeks earlier which had made her very ill and the court concluded that she was in more danger from herself than she was from Golds. It was decided that the arrival of a pregnancy whilst still unmarried had upset the girl and unhinged her mind.

5 Prostitution

Prostitution was a great nuisance for the Victorians and in some of the Kent towns it was virtually impossible for a man to walk around at night without being accosted by various 'loose women'. At the start of the Victorian era prostitutes were generally accepted as part of life and were rarely prosecuted providing they caused no nuisance to ordinary citizens. It was generally accepted that where there was a large barracks, as at Chatham, there were bound to be prostitutes. One early prosecution was of Mary Bauckham of Chatham, who was sentenced to four months in prison for keeping a 'disorderly house' or brothel.

As explained in Fraser Harrison's book, *The Dark Angel*, the prevalence of venereal disease meant that most customers preferred a younger prostitute who was less likely to have contracted something unpleasant. There was therefore quite a lot of pressure on young working girls to become prostitutes, though the Society for the Protection of Young Females did its best to defend them. In 1842 the Society successfully prosecuted eight Chatham publicans who had been involved in a racket whereby young girls from the neighbouring villages were 'procured' on the promise of earning fabulous sums of money. In reality the sort of trade that Chatham offered was unlikely to make any girl rich and most of the town's 'gay women' lived lives only slightly above the standards of the gutter. Most of the activity in the 1840s centred upon 'lodging houses' in Chatham's Brook district, though the West Street area of Gravesend was reckoned to be almost as bad.

It was in the 1890s that prostitution became a big issue in the Kent newspapers which had been encouraged by the crusading work of several London journalists. To reveal what was going on on the streets was brave work, since only a few years had elapsed since the editor of *The Pall Mall Gazette* had been sent to prison for revealing the truth about this shocking trade.

During 1893 there were one hundred and twenty cases of 'lewd' behaviour by women in Chatham alone. 'Lewd' crimes included openly soliciting on the streets, gross indecency in public, and obscene language – all three commonly practised by the prostitutes of The Brook. In January 1894 Alderman Dunstall launched a campaign to clean up the streets of Chatham by demanding that the Police should 'put down all evils such as prostitution and bad language'. There were more than a few people who felt that the Police were suspiciously tolerant of the women's activities.

The first result of the new campaign was that the Police actually organised some 'raids' on disreputable houses in The Brook, most of which posed as 'lodgings'. At the end of January 1894 the house run by Richard and Charlotte Hobbs was raided and prosecution resulted. At the trial one of the Constables reported what they had discovered when they burst in:

> 'In the downstairs room they found three well-known prostitutes and three sailors sitting around the fire, whilst in three upstairs rooms were found women and sailors in bed together, in another instance a civilian being in bed with a woman.'

The Hobbs couple were found guilty of keeping a disorderly house and fined £5, a small sum unlikely to deter them.

A few weeks later the campaign was extended to the publicans of the district when the landlord of *The Shakespeare* in Military Road was convicted of the same offence.

What seems to have particularly annoyed the Chatham Council at its meeting in January 1894 was that numerous women made repeated appearances in Court and yet their behaviour never changed. As if to emphasise the point, that month Emma Slattery made her thirteenth appearance whilst Caroline Copping, another regular, was arrested yet again for using 'very disgusting language' in The Brook. One of the Councillors put his views in a forthright manner:

> 'The evils complained of were open solicitation by lewd women, not restrained by law; the disorderly state of the public streets arising from persons in various stages of intoxication; the filthy and profane language which appeared

to be unchecked; the unrestricted music and dancing in public houses not licensed therefor . . . '

The Police response was to continue their raids on Public Houses. In February 1894 they raided the *Prince Alfred* in Fair Row, Chatham. They found a bargee drunk in the yard, ten drunken men in the bar, several drunken women in a back parlour, one of whom was later found in bed with 'a civilian'. A Constable told the Magistrates that he had seen 'low women frequent the house nightly with different men'; this time the Court acted positively – the landlord lost his licence.

Yet progress in this campaign was very slow. In November 1894 Emma Slattery notched up her sixteenth court appearance – this time for being drunk.

The Tonbridge election riot

CHAPTER FIVE

THE EXCITEMENT OF POLITICS

The Great Reform Bill of 1832 abolished many of the eccentricities of the old constituencies, but there were still comparatively few people who could vote. Thus an election could turn on how one or two men voted and, since there was no secret ballot, Kent newspapers regularly published lists showing how everyone had voted. The vast majority of people, including all women, could not vote at all but nonetheless still got very much involved in the proceedings and excitement. This led to quite a few infringements of the law.

The 1837 election was held due to the death of the previous monarch and to mark the ascent of Victoria to the throne. It was the cause of quite a lot of trouble. The linch pins were removed from the wheels of a cart that was being used to convey some Tory voters to the hustings, an action which could have had fatal consequences and which enraged the *Maidstone Journal*, a stoutly Tory paper. Fortunately no-one was killed, but there were several injuries. In Maidstone, 'reformers' demonstrated outside the homes of prominent Tories, giving vent to their feelings by hurling missiles at the windows. But the most serious incident of the election was at Canterbury, where an 'election fracas' involved some street-rioting and the death of John Constant. Constant had been assaulted by George Green, who had beaten him about the head with a piece of wood, causing 'fearful contusions'. The Coroner recorded a verdict of manslaughter.

Queen Victoria was not immediately popular when she came to the throne and, for one reason or another, there were a number of attacks on her during the 1840s. None of these occurred in Kent, but the authorities were very vigilant in chasing up any potential troublemakers. At the end of March 1843 John Richmond was arrested in Chatham for threatening the life of the Queen and also of Sir Robert Peel, the Prime Minister. Inevitably Richmond had made his rash threat in a pub, in a furious response to a girl who had toasted the Queen. Richmond had responded by ranting and raving in a most hostile manner, saying that:

> ' . . . the first opportunity he had he would blow the Queen's brains out, as she was nothing but an impostor, and that a woman had no right to sit on the throne at all. She was tutored by Sir Robert Peel, and that he should blow his brains out or chop his head off with a hatchet.'

At his trial it emerged that Richmond was an old soldier who felt embittered with life and he was remanded in custody whilst the Court contacted the Home Secretary. Richmond eventually escaped without a capital penalty, but only twenty-five years earlier he would have been in grave danger of execution.

Tonbridge was the scene of some of the worst election riots that ever occurred in the County, with notable violence in 1865 and 1880. However it should not be assumed that election riots only took place in the larger towns, for on one occasion Hadlow was the scene of such trouble – much to the terror of the tiny local Police force. In the 1865 election the Conservatives did well and the two seats for the part of the County covering Tonbridge and Tunbridge Wells were held by them. Parties of Tory supporters from these two towns decided to journey to Maidstone to hear the declaration of the poll. This gave the Liberal supporters a chance to give voice to their frustrations, since the Tories always seemed to dominate the County. The more excitable Liberals in Tonbridge therefore prepared to give the Tories an unexpected reception when they returned from Maidstone that night.

By lunchtime of that July day in 1865 plans to give the Tories 'a warm reception' had been drawn up and during lunchtime 'squibs' were posted throughout the town. Refuse in the form of rotten tomatoes and mouldy carrots was collected from the various grocers' shops. The mob of Liberal supporters began to assemble in the middle of the town at about six o'clock in the evening, having learnt that a band was expected to parade through the town between eight and nine o'clock. The Police did nothing, standing around or disappearing altogether. The crowd had little to do and so any carriage that passed by was hooted and jostled, whether connected with the election party or not.

By nine o'clock there was still no sign of the Tories and the crowd gathered outside the Bull Inn and the Town Hall. About two hundred of them charged off along the Hadlow Road, hoping to meet the returning group and waylay them before they entered the town. This advance party was 'armed with missiles of all kinds'. The procession of triumphant Tories arrived in about twelve carriages at half past nine and were greeted with a shower of eggs, sand and even stones. The drivers of the carriages, who were most at risk from this assault anyway, whipped up their horses and escaped by back routes into the top part of the town which was not Liberal 'territory'. However the group from Tunbridge Wells was following close behind and did not have the advantage of local knowledge; they came straight through the town and into the Swan Lane district where the crowd fell upon them with glee. Heads were broken and windows smashed in great numbers, with the Police being notable by their absence.

The Magistrates were later at great pains to absolve the Police from blame, but it will be noted that the plans for the riot had been laid well in advance; the Police had clearly had sufficient time to send for reinforcements but had failed to do so. Four of the rioters were arrested and taken to court, where they were fined £20 each.

There was another election riot at Tonbridge on 6th April 1880. On this occasion the Police were very much involved to the extent that twelve officers, including the Chief Constable, were injured. Again a mob assembled in the town and, lacking a visible opposition, turned their attention to the attendant Police who received a deluge of eggs and flour. The Police then cleared the town and retired, well-satisfied, in the belief that their work was finished. However, a couple of plain-clothes men had been drafted in to wander around and check that all was peaceful, which it was not for long. They hurried back to report that the mob had emerged again and held control in the town centre. On the second occasion it took ninety-four officers to re-establish law and order.

Kent's history is rather short on genuine revolutionaries, but in November 1839 it at last appeared that one had been discovered in the unlikely shape of a Baptist minister from Canterbury. Earlier that year fourteen people had been killed in the famous 'Newport Rising' in Monmouthshire, which was led by the Chartists. The Government acted swiftly to try and quell the trouble with numerous arrests, but several of the leaders managed to escape. Some of them were sentenced to death in their absence. One of these was William Davies, who by 22nd November had found his way to Canterbury where he was given shelter by his uncle, Rev. Davies, who was a Baptist. It was not long before the movements of William Davies were traced and led to the arrests of both the rioter and his uncle. The former was arrested for high treason whilst the latter was committed to the town gaol for harbouring a dangerous criminal. The arrest of a leading clergyman, particularly when involved in such an affair as Chartism, caused a sensation in Canterbury. Rev. Davies was bailed for £100 and the people of the town rapidly rallied to his defence; the authorities soon accepted the commonly held belief that Rev. Davies knew nothing of his nephew's revolutionary activities. William Davies had already been sentenced to death, but this was commuted to transportation for life in December 1839.

The revenge of the discontented labourer

CHAPTER SIX

INCENDIARISM

Nowadays we do not refer to 'Incendiarism' but to Arson, but to the Victorians Incendiarism was a common and very threatening crime. It was a cause of major worry for a farmer who, with his haystack or barn impossible to guard, was an easy prey for the vindictive employee or wandering tramp. The more politically motivated 'Captain Swing' incendiarism struck at the farmer where it hurt him most – in the pocket. Any outbreak of rick-burning was thus viewed very seriously indeed for it was a direct assault on property, on a man's livelihood, and it carried undertones of rebellion.

There was an outbreak of incendiarism at Chalk in October 1837. Autumn was a dangerous time for the farmer, since the harvest had been taken in and the haystacks prepared. It was also the time when casual labourers were laid off and, if a farmer had been unwise or cruel, a man might hit back by starting a fire before leaving the district. This was the case in Chalk, where three fires were started within two hundred yards of each other. All three were started on one night and fire engines had to be called from Gravesend, Rochester and Chatham to attend to the conflagration. The farmer who had suffered accused a thrasher, named John Norton, who had recently been sacked, but Norton had fled.

Another type of crime that involved fire was the method of defrauding an Insurance Company by setting fire to your own premises. In November 1838 a house in Week Street, Maidstone, was burnt down and the couple who owned it – named Pollard – were arrested and charged with arson. They were then committed for trial at the Assizes for attempting to defraud the Kent Fire Insurance Company of £150, which was the insured value of the house and shop of theirs that had been destroyed. The trial attracted a great deal of attention and it was soon revealed that the bringing of the charge was a heartless accusation based on rumours that the couple's business had been failing. It emerged that Mr Pollard was a cripple and that his wife had struggled in a most heroic manner to rescue him from the blaze. The couple were acquitted, expert evidence having shown that the chimney of the house was defective.

Incendiarism seems to have been a popular crime amongst malicious children so introducing a third motive for the crime – the perverted pleasure of the arsonist. An example of this was the setting alight of a haystack at Cobham in 1894, an act committed by an eight-year-old boy from Luddesdown. At his trial quite a lot of evidence emerged as to the unpleasant nature of this boy, including a report that he had been thrown out of Luddesdown school for kicking the schoolmistress. He received six strokes of the birch as a punishment.

Incendiarism, and the fear of it, seemed to go in cycles. This was partly because it reached a peak every autumn and partly because it was a crime that seemed to attract the criminal into repeating his work. In Autumn 1839 there was an outbreak of rick-burning in the Eastry area that displayed all the classic features of this type of crime: it broke out in September, occurred several times and on one occasion involved four haystacks and a large barn at Hearnden, and was all due to one man – John Ranger, who had been working in the district as a casual labourer. Ranger was sent for trial at the Assizes and was transported for life, a severe sentence reflecting the panic that his activities had caused in the Eastry district.

At almost the same time a barn at Otford, belonging to a farmer named Selby, was burnt down. A complicated story of revenge emerged and an eleven year old boy was arrested. Two years previously the boy's brother and an accomplice had robbed one of Mr Selby's workmen and the farmer had brought a prosecution. The elder brother, named Sutton, had been found guilty and sentenced to transportation, though in 1839 he was apparently still on board one of the hulks moored in the Thames. It was alleged that Sutton had incited his younger brother to gain revenge on Selby by burning down his barn, but not enough evidence was produced and the boy was acquitted.

Not far away and the same Autumn, at Shoreham, a disgruntled farmworker got his thirteen-year-old son to burn down a barn belonging to his employer. The boy was duly arrested and punished.

One case of arson was clearly separate from the rest, attracting greater national attention and apparently differing in motive since it became an issue of 'National security'. The event occurred at Sheerness Dockyard in September 1840, at a time when the national press was alive with rumours of war against France. A new naval vessel, the *Camperdown*, was under construction and was virtually complete when a carpenter happened to find that the ship was on fire. The alarm was quickly raised and the flames put out, after which the origin of the blaze was traced to 'a heap of combustibles' which had been piled up on the deck. The news rapidly spread around Sheerness and from there it reached the attention of the national press; but had the fire been started by a malicious workman or through the treachery of an enemy agent? The circumstances of the fire aboard the *Camperdown* were strangely similar to those of a fire on board the *Talavera* at Plymouth, and this seemed to point towards enemy action as the likely cause.

Early in October 1840 two Dockyard workmen, Wright and Grigg, were the chief suspects and both had been arrested. The Lords of the Admiralty arrived to listen to the evidence, but it soon emerged that Wright and Grigg were innocent – there was virtually no evidence against them at all. This deepened the mystery all the more and spy stories gained ready credence – a popular one referred to the sighting of a 'man in a cloak' acting suspiciously in the neighbourhood. There was considerable shock in the district when the carpenter who had discovered the fire, Henty, was himself arrested and charged.

Henty was arrested at first by the civil authorities who, after he had appeared before them, released him; he got as far as the courtroom door before he was arrested again – this time by the naval authorities. He was placed under naval arrest and kept on a ship out at sea. It was expected that Henty would be tried by court-martial in Chatham, but his eventual trial took place on board *HMS Ocean* moored at Sheerness. The confusing pattern of Henty's arrest, acquittal and re-arrest was due to the complicated legal technicalities involved in a case where a civilian workman was accused of having damaged naval property whilst undertaking his duties on the Navy's behalf. But all the discussion proved futile since, at the end of the month, Henty was again released. The Sheerness Spy Mystery was never solved.

More mundane acts of incendiarism were continuing elsewhere. The Cranbrook area was bedevilled by incendiarism in 1843 and 1844, the fires starting shortly after twenty-year-old Will English moved into the district to begin work as a farm labourer. The first fires broke out in November 1843 and then local farmers began to receive threatening letters. One farmer who did was John Unicume, who was informed by post that his oasthouses, barns and haystacks were about to be burnt down. On 7th June 1844 a fire did break out in Unicume's oasthouse and stables; this farmer was the employer of Will English, who was in the area at the time of the blaze and was sent by his boss to summon the Cranbrook fire-engine, an errand over which he did not hurry. After the blaze was put out suspicion focussed on English and a search of his lodgings revealed incriminating letters. These were produced at the trial but the jury ignored them, acquitting English despite all the evidence.

Incendiarism did not usually result in loss of life since farm out-buildings were the usual target. However, in May 1845 Charles Sims was sent to prison for manslaughter after he started a fire in which Thomasin Payne died. This was an unusually well-organised crime in which Sims set fire to a house by soaking mats and blinds with an inflammable liquid called camphine.

Farmers did not often meet the cause of their problems, since the incendiarist usually left the district in fear of discovery. The Ulcombe region was struck by two fires within a few days of each other shortly after the the 1845 harvest. On the first occasion the farmer was sadly surveying the ruins of his buildings when a man ran up to him. 'It's a judgement from God sent upon you,' the unknown man said, then ran away quickly leaving the bemused farmer powerless to chase him. Clearly this was one arsonist who saw himself as an arm of the Almighty.

Random attacks on farm buildings and haystacks declined later in the century, partly because there were fewer wandering labourers and partly due to better policing. During the 1880s though there was a renewed bout of activity, encouraged by the ready availability of 'Lucifer matches', which tempted many children to set fire to haystacks just for fun. One such child who must have caused great embarrassment for his father was Percy Okill, the son of the Sevenoaks District Police superintendent. In the winter of 1883 a haystack burst into flames at Addington; Percy Okill was seen running away from the scene of the crime, across a field. He was chased and caught but protested his innocence; according to young Percy, he had seen a boy with a red scarf set fire to the haystack and had been in the act of chasing the villain when he himself had been apprehended by mistake. The district was searched but no boy with a red scarf was found, so it was concluded that Percy was lying in an effort to save his own skin. Numerous witnesses had seen Percy, but no-one had seen the boy with the scarf. Percy was remanded in custody and later fined.

Any wandering beggar or tramp was a cause of suspicion to a farmer, who might have his haystack set on fire if he refused to provide a meal. Sometimes, though, a tramp started a fire by accident. This happened with an old man named Robert Adams at Luddesdown in 1895. Adams had been drinking heavily and could not manage to walk very far that night, so he made for the nearest haystack and prepared to settle down for the night. He decided to light his pipe and have a smoke before going to sleep, but was so drunk that he dropped the matches and set fire to the haystack. At first there was some suspicion that he had set fire to it on purpose, but at his trial he was let off with a caution.

Incendiarism is one of the crimes that was much talked about in Victorian times but is now relatively rare.

CHAPTER SEVEN

ASSAULT

1 A General Review

Exactly what constituted an 'assault' was not always made clear by Victorian law, but prosecutions for it were nonetheless numerous and very varied. Some of them were also extremely comical. Broadly speaking, something was counted as an assault if one person launched an attack on another with intent to cause physical harm. The seriousness of the offence was determined by the nature of the harm done; as drink played a large part in a number of assault cases, the injury was not always what the assailant had intended.

Assault charges probably rivalled minor theft as the most common cause for appearance in a Kent courtroom. The motives for assault were numerous, but a sordid trio of causes could usually be relied upon: family rows, money and drink.

An example of assault charges having originated from an argument over money can be found in the case of Thomas Kipps, a farmer from Kemsing. In this case the potential money was not represented by cash but by the ownership of a cottage. The cottage in question, apparently a very old one, was the home of a woman named Ellen Barrett. Barrett and Kipps disagreed as to who actually owned the cottage, but Kipps was the more forceful in expressing his views. Despite his menaces, Miss Barrett refused to quit the house and one day in 1839 Kipps and a few helpers suddenly descended on her, removed all her furniture into the garden and locked the door – with the old woman still inside. Even force did not move Barrett and she acted rather in the way of the old ladies who oppose oncoming motorways in our own day. Being locked inside the house, the woman had a problem with food, but this was solved through the kind support of her neighbours who fed her by breaking a window and supplying her needs. After two days of this Kipps felt even more frustrated and returned with his assistants; the woman refused to budge from her chair, so Kipps carried the chair – and the woman – out into the garden and dumped her on the lawn. She had been evicted.

The result of this feud was that the farmer, Kipps, was hauled before the Magistrates accused of assaulting the woman. It is highly likely that the Magistrates themselves were property owners and Kipps appears to have had a favourable hearing. Though he was found guilty he received only a very small fine – one shilling. It is perhaps worth noting that the local people were opposed to him, as shown by their support for Ellen Barrett. But it was the farmers who ruled the County in 1839.

As detailed later, navvies were notorious for their violent escapades and a good number of these ended in court with assault charges. Every so often, after they had been paid, navvies went on a spree for a few days which was known colloquially as a 'randy'. A 'randy' inevitably involved drink after which some navvies at least enjoyed a fight; not surprisingly, therefore, not every publican provided a navvy with a warm welcome. In September 1845 a navvy attempted to enter a pub at Wateringbury, but the publican had other ideas; the result was a struggle in which the navvy smashed his way into the hostelry, only to be arrested shortly afterwards and charged with assaulting the publican. In the same month a navvy waylaid a man in Tunbridge Wells. The navvy, who was accompanied by a dog, circled his victim and then made a grab for the gentleman's umbrella. The man resisted, clinging to his umbrella, and so the navvy launched a furious assault, totally beating him up. The dog also seems to have had some navvy blood, for it joined in the attack and bit the poor man quite severely. The navvy was prosecuted for assault rather than attempted robbery and was given hard labour.

A rather unusual case of assault took place at Greenhithe in August 1847. A wandering labourer named Thomas Carter had entered the County from Essex in the hope of getting some work in the harvesting. He was clearly not in a condition for work, however, since he was so drunk that he had to lie down and sleep – which he did in the middle of the road! Some while later another man, named Carttar, came along on horseback and, seeing a body in the road, his horse shied and nearly threw him. Carter was woken up by the commotion and a furious row erupted between the two men; Carttar lashed out at the drunk with his whip, as a result of which the labourer collapsed. Carttar rode off.

Thomas Carter died and Carttar was later arrested at Dartford. There was some confusion over the arrest, some local newspapers reporting that a senior contractor on the 'London & Rochester Railway' named Dawes was responsible for the crime. In fact Carttar was a blacksmith by trade who had become foreman on the South Eastern Railway works at Dartford. There was some debate over whether the incident constituted assault or manslaughter, showing the narrow line between the two; in fact it was decided that it was more serious than assault since a man had died, however unintentionally. Carttar received a sentence fairly similar to one for assault – six months of hard labour.

A type of transport that has now wholly vanished was the carrier's wagon. This was really the bus service of its day, taking villagers and their produce to market, and was a much slower affair than the stagecoach. A carrier's wagon plying for trade between Maidstone and Marden was at the centre of a farcical assault trial held at Cranbrook in July 1865. The man in charge of the wagon, Horace Stanley, was having a busy day and, leaving Maidstone, his vehicle was nearly overburdened with passengers. This was the background for a case in which Margaret Pankhurst, one of the passengers, accused Stanley of having assaulted her. She alleged that the conditions in the van were so uncomfortable that at the 'Fortune of War' public house she got up and sat on the footboard of the van. According to Pankhurst, Stanley was so angry about this that he grabbed hold of her and threw her into a hedge. This was the basis for the charge, but at the trial Stanley was able to produce a witness who claimed that Pankhurst had started the argument by kicking Stanley and the case was dismissed amidst laughter.

A number of assault charges featured women who, as neighbours, had had too much of each other. Typical was Laura Allen of Higham who, in 1894, was fined five shillings for throwing a pail of dirty water over her neighbour.

A more complicated neighbourly row took place at Herne Bay in 1866. Ann Appleton was charged with assaulting Sarah Webb, the assault weapon again being a pail of water. In fact the pail of water was only one stage in a long and bitter contest between the two women, which also included a lawsuit against Webb for abusive language. The two women both had homes in Salt Lane, where they shared the use of a yard and garden. The yard was at the centre of a dispute as to who could put their washing where, and on the day of the incident Ann Appleton was hanging up her dripping clothes when Sarah Webb intervened. 'You shall not dry there,' the latter shouted, but Appleton insisted that it was the same place she always used. To counter this, Webb took direct action – she untied the washing-line and let Appleton's clothes fall onto the dirty ground. Webb followed this by throwing the water over her rival, calling out angrily, 'There, you . . . , take that. And if you want anymore I'll give it to you'. The end result of this little fracas was that Webb was fined one shilling for the assault and ordered to pay another nine shillings costs.

Another unusual assault trial took place in Dover in 1894. A soldier in the King's Royal Rifles thought he would play a joke on a friend and put some gunpowder in the friend's pipe, covering it over with tobacco to hide it. The mixture exploded, causing serious injury to his friend's face and eyes.

In 1895 a South Eastern Railway telegraph clerk at Ashford was also assaulted in an unusual manner. Whilst dealing with a lady customer, Emma Shaw from London, he was surprised to find himself suddenly under attack and the woman stabbed him with her pen before running off. It was later discovered that the woman, who came from a respectable family, was of unsound mind.

One night in April 1896 the Night Mail cart along the old Watling Street came across a group of people watching a fight in the road near Sittingbourne. The sudden appearance of the cart disrupted the contest and forced the crowd to move hurriedly out of the way, because of which one man fell against the cart and hurt himself. The blood of the crowd was already high because of the excitement of the fight and they were now incensed at the disturbance. The Mail Cart was attacked, with one of its crew being dragged to the ground and brutally kicked. The driver was also assaulted. The crowd then fled into the night and none of the attackers was caught.

2 Prize-Fighting

Prize-fighting was really a form of organised and systematic assault, in which two men were set to beat each other until one collapsed through exhaustion or wounds. It was fairly common for severe injuries to result and the death of one of the 'pugilists' was not unknown. The practice was therefore illegal, but it remained highly popular throughout the Victorian era. Fights were great occasions

The Prize-Fighters

for gambling men and inevitably attracted large crowds; thus they were impossible to hold in London, where the Police would soon track them down. The prize-fighting fraternity therefore made regular journeys into Kent; at first they travelled by Thames steamer, putting up the ring in some remote part of the Kent marshes, whilst later on they could also choose to travel by train. These fights were no small time affair, for they often attracted several thousand spectators and a great deal of money was involved; some of the spectators would also be gentry or, on occasions, members of the aristocracy.

A typical fight was held on the marshes near Greenhithe in December 1843. It had been organised very carefully beforehand, with all the spectators coming down from London on board the steamer *Nymph* equipped with copious supplies of alcohol. The fight was arranged between Taas Parker and the 'Tipton Slasher', with a purse of one hundred sovereigns. It started just after lunch at one o'clock and, to quote an attendant reporter, 'continued with savage barbarity' for one and a half hours. Half a dozen Policemen arrived from Woolwich to quell the disturbance, but they were powerless to do anything when faced with a mob of over three hundred fight supporters. The illegal fight was only stopped by the arrival of three more Police on horseback and a dragoon, who cut through the crowd and slashed the ropes around the ring. This led the reporter to comment, with respect to the earlier failure of the Police, that 'One pair of heels is worth two pairs of hands'.

Prize-fighting still had a form of respectability about it due to its 'sporting' origins and the interest of some of the upper classes. It is notable, therefore, that when another fight was held at Greenhithe almost exactly a year later the County Magistrates refused to interfere; this meant that the Police could not call upon the Army for assistance. The fight of December 1844 was clearly organised by the same people, since it took place in the same place and also used the services of the *Nymph*, supplemented on this occasion by a steam tug called *William Gunston*.

The fight was between Joseph Row and Henry Broom and was preceded by a lively period of discussion and the placing of bets. It started about two o'clock in the afternoon and continued for over two and a half hours, by which time it was dusk and the crowd were losing patience. The mob therefore broke into the ring and stopped the fight, both fighters getting roughed up by the supporters of the opposing man. There was apparently some suspicion that Rowe's supporters had commenced the invasion of the ring because they suspected that their man was on the brink of defeat. At this point the Police arrived, but the mob was not particularly unruly and the officers felt it prudent to refrain from making any arrests. Greenhithe marshes were rather remote from any form of help should a riot occur!

A few months later a fight was scheduled to take place on the marshes near Northfleet but had to be postponed because one of the pugilists had been arrested on a charge of robbery whilst staying in Gravesend. However a prize-fight took place in Chatham in 1846, as a result of which the town was condemned as being 'notorious for vice and profligacy'.

The consequences of a prize-fight were occasionally very tragic. On 11th December 1855 a fight was arranged on the river marshes near Dartford between Michael Madden – who was famous for his shaved head – and John Jones. As usual the spectators were brought down from London by river steamer, stepping ashore at the Long Reach Tavern – thus solving the usual problem of these battle sites, a lack of alcohol on tap. A ring was formed by driving stakes into the ground and stringing ropes between them. Jones prepared for the fight by drinking his usual pre-contest beverage, a mixture of brandy and cocoa; Madden conferred with his assistant, Alexander Noon. Eventually the fight began and it was Jones who gradually gained the upper hand. Jones was clearly winning when he lost his footing on the slippery, wet grass, and stumbled; he fell heavily and hit his head on one of the stakes, knocking himself unconscious. The insensible Jones was carried into the Long Reach Tavern where he died at two o'clock the next morning.

The death of a fighter was a serious affair that could not be hidden from the Police, with the result that Madden and Noon were charged with the unlawful killing of Jones. But juries were still sympathetic to the sporting fraternity and they threw out the charges altogether; Jones had died, they thought, because he had slipped over and not because of Madden's actions. The Police were probably unwise to have prosecuted for Unlawful Killing rather than plain assault, which Madden was clearly guilty of.

A few years later the prize-fight organisers forsook the Thames steamers in favour of the railway and it is fairly certain that the railway companies did nothing to discourage them. In 1859 trains with over two thousand spectators on board left London by courtesy of the South Eastern Railway and headed down its Dover main-line, looking for a field in which to hold a fight. The trains stopped between Headcorn and Pluckley, presumably in a siding, and a series of fights were held. The third fight of the day was in progress when the Police arrived and broke up the proceedings. The South Eastern Railway received a severe rebuke from the Home Secretary.

The South Eastern assisted with the arrangements for another fight in 1861. On this occasion they ran an excursion from London Bridge to Strood, from where the fight-goers picked up the ferry *Jupiter* which took them to a remote island in the middle of the Medway estuary. The Police reaction to this was too slow to stop the fight.

The London, Chatham & Dover Railway was a party to the breaking of the law concerning another fight in 1861. That company had just opened its line from Pimlico to Chatham and an excursion was run down this route as far as Meopham to hold a fight between two men named Brettle and Rooke. Again this was no small affair, with a purse of £1,000. However Police from Rochester and Dartford soon arrived to interrupt the proceedings and everyone got back on the train. They all carried on down the line looking for another place to hold the fight, the train carrying on to Milton Meads near Sittingbourne. There everyone got out again; Police were present, but the crowd had become so hostile that they did not intervene.

3 **Assaults in Church**

For some strange reason, church and religious issues occasioned a number of assaults quite contrary to the philosophy of the Christian faith. An example of quite irreligious conduct was displayed by William Thompson, who was Parish Clerk at Frindsbury in 1894. Thompson had an official seat in the front pew of his Parish Church and some people felt that this honour had made him impossibly pompous. One woman who clearly felt so was Mary Johnson. When Mary Johnson's nephew was to get married, Johnson clearly felt that she had a right – through her family connection – to sit in the front pew, but Thompson disagreed. He asked her to vacate his pew, but she refused. Thompson's response was to lock the church door so that the bride could not get in until the woman gave up the seat.

The dispute did not stop there. In October 1894 Mary Johnson's niece got married and virtually the same things happened as before. Johnson again took up a position in Thompson's official pew, the Parish Clerk again ordered her out and once more she refused. This time he tried to drag her out, there was a scuffle and Thompson caused Johnson to sprain her wrist. She brought an assault charge against him and he was fined fourteen shillings.

More usually the violence took place outside the church. With the spread of nonconformism it became quite likely that a couple might have different views as to which church or chapel to attend. In April 1845 a Staplehurst labourer knocked down and kicked his wife for going to a place of worship that he disapproved of. He threatened to repeat the punishment if she disobeyed him again, but received a punishment himself when he was fined for the assault.

Pews were again the issue at Hythe in 1866. On Sunday evening, 18th March, Charles Nelson and Kate Godfrey went to church. When they had taken up their position in a pew of their choice, Mr and Mrs Oliver Hole arrived and wished to use the same pew. Nelson refused and exactly what happened next was lost in a confusion of claim and counter-claim. Nelson stated that Mrs Hole leaned over and pulled his whiskers, whilst she claimed that he pushed her away most severely. However it was Mrs Hole who won the struggle, since she went into the pew behind Nelson and climbed over the top, so achieving her aim of getting into his pew. After the service they all issued a summons against each other but, in court, it was Nelson who lost; he was fined one pound six shillings for assaulting Mrs Hole.

One case that got nowhere occurred in Dover in 1843. A churchwarden had the duty of seeing that everyone who attended church did so in a 'sober and orderly' manner, as stipulated by the statute of Queen Elizabeth I. One of the Dover churchwardens was intensely annoyed to find a publican sitting in church during a service with his hat on and smartly whisked the offending article off the man's head. The publican was most upset by this and brought a civil action against the churchwarden, contending that the unauthorised removal of his hat constituted an assault. The case was thrown out as soon as it reached court.

4 Self-Inflicted Assault – the Prosecution of Attempted Suicides

Throughout the Victorian period it was a criminal offence to attempt suicide, so it was always possible that someone who tried and failed would be punished severely rather than given help with their problems. In practice the judiciary were generally fairly lenient with this law, very rarely using it to inflict punishment but more often finding it a way to ensure that someone was well looked after. Nonetheless a suicide or an attempted suicide was still regarded with considerable gravity, since many believed that a suicide would spend eternity in Hell.

The suicide of an old couple at Stodmarsh in April 1838 was thus reported by the *Maidstone Journal* with due solemnity. The depressed old folk had killed themselves by putting arsenic into their hot apple pie and new bread.

A more scandalous event shook Ramsgate in August 1837. For some time the looser members of the town's bar-room society had been enjoying the attentions and talents of a young girl who had arrived in the town a few months before. The girl was very attractive and had soon established a career as a bar-room singer; according to a local newspaper, her 'society was greatly courted by the gay part of the visitors'. This was a subtle reference to her activities, since 'gay woman' was a common Victorian euphemism for prostitute. However it turned out that the girl had her origins in the 'polite society' of upper middle-class London and, eventually, her parents tracked her down to Ramsgate. The girl, who had by now had a good taste of freedom, refused to return to London with them and tried to escape along the pier of the resort. Realising that she was trapped, the girl threw herself despairingly into the sea from which she was promptly rescued by a local mariner. According to the press, the girl was then reconciled with her parents and returned to London quite happily. It is notable that this attempted suicide did not end with a prosecution; social class was a useful defence against the law, whatever the crime.

The law changed very little throughout Victoria's reign in this respect, so that by the 1890s attempted suicides were still being punished, though it was by then less customary to despatch them post haste to the workhouse or the asylum. One woman who was treated leniently was Edith Goodenough, who tried to end her life in January 1894. Edith was clearly a fairly simple woman who had little comprehension of the marriage laws and this had led to her feeling depressed and rejected. Edith had been living with a man at Chalk for seven years and had had a child by him; the couple had never been properly married, but the man's mother had told Edith that they counted as man and wife because of a 'licence'. However, Edith's mother-in-law (if that's what she was!) also told the poor woman that one of these licences was only valid for seven years, after which the couple ceased to be man and wife. Inevitably, as soon as the seven years were up, the man left Edith and went to live in Cliffe with his mother.

Poor Edith was left desolate and distressed. Lost in her misery she took a walk along the banks of the old Thames & Medway Canal, which near Chalk ran parallel to the Gravesend to Strood railway line. The cold, still water offered

Edith the possibility of escape from her misery and so she jumped in, determined to drown. However Henry Carvell, watching from a distance, saw the woman fall into the water and rushed to the rescue; he succeeded in dragging her out. Edith's misery was then further compounded by being brought before the Magistrates, charged with attempted suicide. She tried to defend herself by saying that two trains had gone past and given her such a shock that she had fallen into the Canal, but this was an unconvincing story. She was remanded in custody for a week, largely for her own protection, and on her second court appearance her father appeared and promised to look after her. Edith Goodenough was taken home in his care.

Another person who attempted suicide that year was Henry Green of Luton. Green was an unstable young man who tried to cut his own throat, but only injured himself. When brought before the Magistrates he fainted away and they had to pause in the hearing. They could find no reason for punishing him. Less lucky in a way was Alice Archer, a thirty-six year old washerwoman from Snodland. She tried to drown herself in the River Medway but was dragged out and punished with seven months of hard labour.

A young man from Chatham was involved in a most sensational case in January 1894. Jasper was a confectioner from Chatham whose sexual tastes were clearly not of the type approved by the Victorian press, which had difficulty in describing his relationship with a young man from Hastings called Stower; in the end the Editor chose to describe the two young men as 'most intimate friends'. Jasper was in the habit of visiting Stower and it was as a result of one of these visits that the two young men were found – both dead and both in the same bed. All sorts of rumours circulated as to what had happened but it was discovered that both young men, as well as being intimate friends, were also morphia addicts. They had been in the room together and had been giving each other doses of the drug, when Stower had accidentally administered too large a dose to his friend with fatal results. Unable to face the scandal and life without his friend, Stower then killed himself with a poison called aconite.

5 Assault Against the Ear – Bad Language

The Victorian magistrates viewed the speaking of obscene words very seriously, especially if they were used to the public nuisance in the street. In practice obscene language was usually associated with two other crimes – drunkenness and prostitution. The Chatham prostitutes were regularly summonsed throughout the 1890s on account of their bad language, usually referred to as 'lewd', but this seems to have been used to add variety to the charges that they normally faced. Strangely enough it was nearly always women who appeared on obscene language charges!

A typical example was Elizabeth O'Hara of Best Street, Rochester, who in 1894 was fined the large sum of fourteen shillings for using bad language in the street. This caused a local journalist to enjoy himself with puns on 'best', referring to being on her 'best' behaviour when out in the street. Best Street was notorious as a centre of depravity in Rochester.

These charges were repeated with monotonous regularity and were rarely unusual or interesting. The same people appeared in court over and over again. In July 1874 Caroline Brown made her twentieth visit to the Gravesend Court when she was charged with being drunk – another offence for which prostitutes were commonly arrested. The Magistrates sentenced her to twenty-eight days in gaol, which clearly did not please her at all since, on hearing it, she directed a torrent of abusive language at the Bench. This led to another appearance in Court – charged with the use of abusive language in Court! Throughout this second hearing the foolish woman behaved most defiantly and again directed a string of obscenities at the learned residents of the Bench, who were not at all pleased. They showed their feelings by sentencing Brown to an extra month in gaol, which at least kept her out of the way for a few weeks.

6 Two Typical Assault Cases

To conclude this chapter we can have a look at two contrasting assault cases in a little more detail. It is generally true to say that the most frequent causes of assault were drunkenness and pure, personal spitefulness. These two cases demonstrate how this sort of thing happened – with what must have seemed monotonous regularity to the ever-patient Magistrates.

In October 1865 there was a brawl at the 'Plough Inn' in Ightham which ended with six men in custody – quite a fair number for a small village! The Publican, John Harding, said that he was serving drinks as usual when a group of men – who had been drinking heavily – started quarrelling. For a while it looked as if they might just shout, but then they started scuffling and, which most annoyed Harding, breaking the furniture. Harding attempted to stop the fight, but his intervention succeeded only in channelling their fury into an onslaught on himself. One of the brawlers hit him in the eye and another 'kicked him upon the lower part of his person'. The brawl broke out into a general fracas and the village Constable was sent for; he arrived to find two men with their shirts off, and was promptly assaulted himself. One man thumped the policeman, another pulled his coat off and a third kicked him. A man named Murphy pulled the leg off a stool and hit the Constable with it. By the time the riot had been quelled there were six men in custody, all of whom were later sentenced to six weeks' hard labour.

An altogether different assault case involved William Jarman, a bootmaker of Jeffrey Street, Gillingham, who was arrested in 1893. Jarman employed a seventy-year-old assistant named Herbert Sheldrake who clearly did not work as hard as Jarman wanted him to. Jarman attacked the old man because of his fury, 'seized him by the throat, struck him and then threw a boot at him which hit him on the head'. Sheldrake brought charges against Jarman, but the bootmaker tried to provide a defence for himself by getting a ten-year-old boy to give evidence on his behalf. This did not please the Magistrate at all: 'the Magistrate said that the defendant had aggravated his misconduct by calling a miserable little boy with the intention of deceiving the court'. Jarman was fined two pounds for the assault, then was brought back into court since he owed Sheldrake ten shillings and sixpence in pay; he was made to hand it over.

CHAPTER EIGHT

RIOTOUS ASSEMBLY

The social life of any Victorian community was always prone to being turbulent and the old-fashioned riot was very much part of the scene. In days when education was only for a handful and the ballot box was available to even fewer, the riot was one of the few ways in which people of the lower classes could express their feelings and frustrations. Riots generally had two forms of inspiration: they were either motivated by some political or economic discontent, or they sprang out of high spirits and drunkenness.

1 The Boughton Messiah

The strange and bizarre events surrounding the career of the 'Boughton Messiah', John Thom, and the culmination of his political campaign were probably the most important events to take place in Kent politics during the Victorian age. Whatever the initial stimulus behind Thom, most of his supporters were motivated by a political aim – the destruction of the workhouse. At the end of his career, fourteen people had died because of Thom's actions, the biggest single breakdown of law and order in Kent during the last two hundred years and one of the most serious rural riots that have taken place in England since 1800.

Various historians have observed that the years of 1837-8 witnessed a number of anti-workhouse riots in the North of England, some of which were serious enough for the troops to be called out. Less interest has been shown in how the agricultural workers of the South reacted, though labourers in counties like Kent were threatened by low wages and the loss of security.

The idea of the workhouse had been championed by Edwin Chadwick, the architect of the new Poor Law of 1834. The basic idea was to stop people from applying for poor relief unless they were absolutely desperate in order to check the abuses of old methods of payment like the Speenhamland system. Chadwick's solution was to make payments available only to people who surrendered their liberties and took a place inside the workhouse – where husbands and wives were separated and life might involve constant toil with only a faint hope of relief from its misery. Chadwick believed that life inside the workhouse should be substantially less pleasant than any form of employment outside of it, thus hoping to discourage shirkers. In practice the system was far from successful.

The problem in Kent was that much of the work, which was mostly still agricultural in the 1830s, was seasonal. Thus it was likely that a man might be unemployed for part of the year, during which time he had to feed his family somehow. The New Poor Law threatened to withdraw the system of 'outdoor relief', under which a man could claim assistance yet remain in his own home. The new plan, the workhouse, offered a long-term solution to what was only a short term problem since the poor were not allowed to wander in and out of the workhouse according to how the employment market fluctuated. A man either had to take his family into the workhouse for a lengthy stay, or take a chance and starve at home. Not surprisingly, many workers saw the workhouse as a dark and brooding threat to their liberty.

The Parishes of Kent were organised into groups for the purposes of operating a joint workhouse; these groups were called a Union. Each Union built its own workhouse, one of the most notorious being at Herne where the building had no outside windows. Once a person was admitted, they could see no more of the normal world until they were eventually released; it was a dismal situation and many were prepared almost to starve before they would consider an application to the Poor Law Guardians who ran the workhouse. Into this tense and troubled atmosphere came a strange and tormented man, John Thom.

John Thom was a native of St Columb Major in Cornwall, where he was born in about 1805. He later moved to Kent, where he had relatives, but in October 1833 was sent to the Kent County Lunatic Asylum near Maidstone after having been convicted of perjury. He was released from the Asylum exactly four years later, his father having guaranteed to keep him under close supervision; the circumstances of Thom's release caused considerable controversy in later years.

After his release Thom took to calling himself 'Sir William Courtenay', also claiming the titles of 'King of Jerusalem' and 'Knight of Malta'. His father did little about him, so 'Courtenay' went to live with a farmer named Francis, who lived at Boughton in Kent. This was a remote and backward part of the County, not far from the infamous Herne workhouse.

The name of 'Thom' was now dropped and the rather unsettled young man became generally known as 'Courtenay'. His movements between October 1837 and March 1838 are not well-documented, but we know that he was based for most of this time at Boughton and made regular visits to Canterbury. He began a new career as a political agitator, funded by Francis and also by the farmer's sister-in-law, who had apparently fallen in love with him. At first his political activities were confined to Canterbury where he published a broadsheet named 'The British Lion'; his main policy was to advocate the destruction of all workhouses, though he also showed some sympathy for the union activities of the farm labourers. On account of this second interest, he spent part of the winter of 1837-8 touring the villages between Canterbury and Faversham, speaking to farm labourers, the unemployed and their wives. It was at this time that he began to take advantage of the credulity of these uneducated and often virtually starving people by adding fanciful colouring to his political speeches. Courtenay clearly had an ability with words and he found that he could soon win the confidence of the working people he addressed. Thus he began to claim that he was the Messiah and promised to call down fire from Heaven to destroy all the workhouses and also the City of Canterbury. He reinforced his messianic claims by creating his own stigmata: he made marks on his hands, feet and sides to represent Christ's nail and spear wounds. Courtenay found many prepared to believe him and by early 1838 his followers numbered over a hundred.

However, in Spring 1838 Courtenay fell foul of Francis and was thrown out of his house; this was quite probably because the farmer had begun to dislike the drift of his guest's pronouncements. Francis' sister-in-law maintained her devotion, though, and continued to supply him with money. Courtenay went to live among his impoverished followers, constantly haranguing them about the Poor Law. According to one report he also drilled them in military order.

Access to money, good oratory and a cause that was deeply felt amongst the local poor enabled Courtenay to build up his support with eventually tragic consequences. Fear of the workhouse, and a desperate desire to do anything but submit to its inhumanity, gave him a resource to draw on of frightened and unthinking persons. On 27th May 1838 he collected a large band of his supporters together near the village of Ospringe and plied them with beer. Then they marched through the village with Courtenay at the front, apparently unafraid of the authorities, the *Maidstone Journal* commented of his supporters that '. . . many of them were so miserably and awfully deluded as to believe that he had the power of rendering them incapable of receiving injury from sabres or bullets'. Sadly, Courtenay soon proved unable to protect even himself.

The following day over forty of his followers gathered at Boughton and then marched to Fairbrook. There a loaf was put on top of a pole, the clear inference being that the starving people demanded bread; despite its weird pretences, the Boughton 'crusade' was, at heart, an old-fashioned bread riot. Next to the loaf they tied a flag of blue and white, with a picture of a lion. Courtenay then marched the group to Goodnestone, near Faversham, and from there to a farm at Herne-Hill where Courtenay forced the farmer to provide food and drink for the whole group. The farmer had no real choice in the matter. The ragged army carried on from there to Dargate Common where Courtenay made a strange declaration; taking off his shoes, he announced, 'I now stand on my own bottom'. A curious statement. The Messiah concluded the day with a prayer meeting and then they all slept in a barn at Bossenden.

On 29th May Courtenay was up at 3 a.m. and led his followers through the dawn mist to Sittingbourne. They spent the day on an apparently aimless trek around a variety of villages, passing through Newnham, Eastling, Throwley, Sheldwich, Lees and Selling before ending up back at Bossenden, where they slept another night in the barn.

30th May marked the culmination of Courtenay's 'campaign'. The village Constable at Boughton, Mears, was called out to go and arrest a servant who had absconded to join the Messiah's disciples. The Constable's brother, Nicholas, volunteered to accompany him on account of the considerable danger involved. When the two men got to Bossenden Wood, Courtenay replied to the challenge swiftly – he shot dead Nicholas Mears, then lunged at the Constable with a knife.

The latter escaped only because Courtenay missed with his first effort and then tripped over whilst giving chase to the fleeing Constable.

The threat to authority had now become clear. Not only was Courtenay challenging the Poor Law, he was also on the point of inspiring a general revolt against the wealthier residents of the locality. So the local gentry began to gather on horseback within the vicinity of Bossenden Wood, though they did not attempt to approach the group who by now numbered fifty persons – none of whom had a horse. A detachment of the 45th Regiment was summoned from Canterbury and one hundred soldiers arrived under the command of Major Armstrong. Courtenay formed his followers into a defensive square, at the middle of which were a female trumpeter and the flag. It seemed that he intended to turn the occasion into a full-scale battle.

Accompanying Major Armstrong was a Lieutenant Bennett, who had volunteered to come along with the rest of the troops. This officer approached Courtenay and attempted to talk to him. The 'Messiah's' response was to shoot at him, but on this occasion he missed; however, one of his followers also took aim and shot the officer dead. George Catt of Faversham, who had enlisted as a Special Constable, then tried to grapple with the lunatic leader but was shot in the head and also died. Meanwhile, Major Armstrong was trying to persuade the assembled gentry and their wives to retreat, since there was a real danger that the spectators could be hit by stray bullets.

Such was Courtenay's belligerence, and his hold over his followers, that there was no alternative except a direct assault by the Army. When the troops charged, Courtenay himself was one of the first victims, being first shot in the arm by a sergeant and then bayonetted to death by another soldier. Armstrong had clearly expected the death of the leader to cause the others to give up, but this was not to be the case. Instead there ensued a vicious struggle that ended with six of the rioters lying dead, another four mortally wounded, and twenty-nine arrested. Thus the Boughton Messiah's campaign had caused fourteen deaths.

The bodies were taken to an inn at Dunkirk and laid out in the stables with their heads beneath the mangers. The situation remained tense, with hysterical women weeping in the street and vowing that Courtenay would return from the dead to claim vengeance. Many of these women had been present at the battle. A reporter commented, 'One of the wretches who died from his wounds expired expressing the belief that Courtenay was his saviour! A woman whose son was shot declared that she would be happy to suffer martyrdom for Courtenay'.

Rumours circulated wildly, particularly as to the identity of Courtenay, but it was several days before the truth was announced. Other people wanted to know how much the farmer, Francis, had been involved; it was reported that Courtenay had taken his followers to the nearby farm for gin and water after the shooting of the Constable. However, Francis managed to emerge from the various debates without blame.

Fourteen of the prisoners were taken to Maidstone gaol for trial at the Kent Assizes in August, twelve of them on murder charges. But it was no longer a purely Kent affair, being debated first by Brougham and Melbourne and then by the House of Commons in June 1838. At first discussion centred on 'Courtenay' and how he had been allowed to go free, but there was also the danger of further outbreaks of violence in Kent to concern the Government since many of his supporters had escaped. Thus during 1838 the Government had to worry about anti-Poor Law riots in both the North and the South of the country.

Reports conflict on what type of person actually supported Courtenay. The earliest accounts suggested that most of his followers were in steady farm jobs, but these reports were later amended to place an emphasis on the unemployed. Of the fourteen taken to Maidstone gaol, less than half were in work. They were clearly from the class most threatened by the Poor Law and most gave Courtenay's denunciation of the workhouse as the reason for following him. One of the prisoners had had his tongue and teeth shot out, so there was popular speculation as to how he would give evidence.

Most of the prisoners were found guilty of murder, but it is highly significant that none were executed. Two were transported for life, one for ten years, and six received one year's hard labour. By the standards of the time these were mild punishments and it may well be that they were a considered reaction to a tense situation. It is interesting to note that there was considerable panic in Canterbury the following year when a Chartist rioter from Wales was arrested there.

The gentry and aristocracy of Kent survived the 'revolution' of Boughton, but it had certainly sent a tremor of fear through the complacent corridors of authority.

2 The Ramsgate Fish Riot

A most unusual riot took place in Ramsgate in July 1839. At the time the town authorities were trying to establish Ramsgate as a genteel and fashionable resort, but were finding that this ambition conflicted with several local traditions and practices. One of the problems for the town authorities was the number of hawkers who constantly plied pedestrians with all manner of goods for sale, thus effectively ruining the peace and quiet desired by those out strolling on the seafront. Therefore in the summer of 1839 a bye-law was passed that prohibited hawking.

This new law had an unfortunate, though probably intentional, effect on one section of the community – it directly threatened the livelihood of those fishermen who sold their fish on the streets. Many of the fish hawkers were not locally based, but originated from as far afield as Devon. The result, inevitably, was a direct clash between the law and those who saw that one section of the community (the hoteliers) were seeking to profit at the expense of another, less politically active, section.

Within a few days of the new law being introduced, a number of the fish hawkers were despatched to the gaol at Sandwich. Generally speaking, those found guilty were offered a choice between a small fine or six days in prison; most chose the prison sentence rather than show acceptance for what they considered to be an unjust law by paying the fine. The initial, rather lenient, sentences only acted as an encouragement to others and there was another series of arrests. This time the various hawkers were either fined one shilling or sent to prison for eight to eighteen days each.

As the second series of trials took place in Ramsgate, an angry mob gathered outside the building. According to one report there were something like a thousand protesters, many of whom were Torbay fishermen and their wives – for this was a matter which affected the whole fishing family. At the end of the legal proceedings, those who had opted for gaol sentences were herded into a van for the journey to Sandwich gaol; a considerable irony was that the prison van was in fact a fish van that had been pressed into rather novel service! Such was the size and mood of the mob that the authorities were powerless to stop their attack on the prison van; they stopped it, broke it open and freed the grateful prisoners who ran off into the crowd. The mob then gave further vent to their anger by hurling missiles at the various buildings around them, including any building that was official or an hotel.

The next hour or so can only be described as a quite uncontrolled outburst of popular disgust for the law and the people who implemented it. The mob, still in a frenzy, rampaged through the middle of Ramsgate, chanting slogans and smashing windows. The authorities were quite unprepared for this and only seven or eight policemen were on duty; they very wisely hid themselves in back yards and alleyways where the crowd would not find them.

After a few troubled hours the riot faded away as the crowd became exhausted. The Ramsgate fish riot had no long term repercussions, but it did show that 'authority' in an early Victorian town was a rather tenuous matter that could easily be overturned should a number of the populace disagree with the policies of those who controlled the local government.

3 The Light Dragoons v. The Canterbury Police

During the 1840s the concept of the Police was still rather novel and in many areas the Police Force was often understaffed and rather weak. It was still general to call out the military whenever public order was threatened and this was usually done with the sanction of the local Magistrates. The Police themselves were not popular with the general public and many of the early officers suffered a good deal of abuse in return for low wages. The maintenance of order was thus made considerably more difficult if the cause of the initial problem was the Army itself, as proved to be the case at Canterbury in April 1841.

The garrison at Canterbury was made up from the soldiers of the Light Dragoons, whose commanding officer was Lord Brudenell; this nobleman had bought control of the Regiment in 1836 for over £40,000. Brudenell later inherited the title of Lord Cardigan and became infamous for his role in the Charge of the Light Brigade during the Crimean War. He was, however, largely unsuited to the role of a commanding officer, being motivated by personal vanity and a desire to be at the forefront of fashion; during the period of 1836-8 he thus replaced many of his more seasoned officers with rash but well-bred young men from London society.

The officers of the 11th Light Dragoons soon earned themselves a degree of notoriety. In August 1838 six of them took a cross-country gallop across the fields of a Mr Brent, an influential Canterbury citizen. Brent tried to tackle the intruders but they galloped away, so he followed them to Canterbury Barracks where his protests were rudely pushed aside. The affair reached the attention of the nation because of the interest in it shown by the *Morning Chronicle* and Lord Cardigan's name suffered a further tarnishing.

This incident was but a prelude to an event of April 1841 when another group of Light Dragoons showed that they were prepared openly to flout the laws of the land. One evening that month a local Constable attempted to arrest Captain Doherty of the Light Dragoons. As the policeman was trying to lead him away, some other officers came to the rescue and dealt the Constable some rough treatment. However, some of the citizens of Canterbury were not enamoured of the vain soldiers and so some bystanders came to the assistance of the Constable. One of the Light Dragoons, Captain Allgood, tried to bribe the policeman with a crown in exchange for the release of his friend, but the Constable was not to be corrupted. As Doherty was led away, Allgood went searching for more soldiers and, with their help, launched an assault on Canterbury Police Station. Thirty or forty soldiers smashed their way into the building and forced open the lock-up with iron crowbars. Doherty was able to escape to the sanctuary of the barracks, with three other officers who had assisted in the rescue.

The next day the City of Canterbury was in uproar. The Light Dragoons had clearly broken the law in several ways and yet it appeared that they had got away with it. The Magistrates and the Police responded to this challenge most forcefully and in some quarters there were demands for courts-martial. Charges were issued against four captains of the Light Dragoons, accusing them of rioting, but it was necessary to identify the criminals and this could only be done if the civil authorities were granted access to the Barracks. The Police contacted Colonel Townsend and requested that the Dragoons be paraded for identification, but at first the Colonel refused. After further pressure was put on him, Townsend relented and several witnesses were allowed in to inspect the Regiment. They were accompanied by the Mayor of Canterbury, but not one of the rioters was identified. In an action undoubtedly orchestrated by the furious Colonel, a sentry then ejected the Mayor from the Barracks at gunpoint.

The Police suspected, correctly, that the ringleaders of the riot had been withheld from the parade. Rumours circulated that the Dragoons were leaving for India in May and that the offenders were being protected until then. However, the Army authorities did not wish to see a second clash between military and civil authority, so on this occasion the Light Dragoons had to climb down.

The four offenders were handed over for trial before the civil authorities and fined between £20 and £50 each in July 1841.

The navvy riot at Markbeech

4 Navvy Riots

The 'Navigators' who built the canals and their successors, the Navvies, who built the railways were well-known for their riotous lifestyle and heavy drinking. The navvies were outsiders in whatever community they visited and the bad reputation that went before them usually resulted in an unfriendly, if not actually hostile, reception. Any crime that occurred whilst a railway was being built through a district was normally blamed on the navvies, whatever the evidence. Navvy work was hard and dangerous, but the navvies lived their leisure hours in much the same way; there were frequent fights between different groups, often based upon where the navvies originated from – England, Scotland, Wales or Ireland.

One of the problems with navvies was that their work depended upon the weather. If there was a period of bad weather, for example heavy rainfall during the winter months, the navvies were laid off and were forced to find other means of feeding themselves. This generally put extra pressure on local resources, with the result that a lot of parishes refused to have anything to do with poor relief for navvies.

An example of this occurred at Mereworth in February 1844. Some twenty or thirty 'excavators' (as the local press called them) had been put out of work, but because they were strangers to the district were refused assistance by the local Relieving Officer who administered the Poor Law. The irate navvies responded by laying siege to the Relieving Officer's home. They encircled the house, threatened to murder him if he did not 'relieve' them, broke windows and held the man captive for four hours. Eventually the Police arrived and four of the navvies were arrested, receiving two months hard labour each. It was not a serious incident, but it revealed the threat that a group of angry navvies could form to law and order in rural districts.

One of the most serious navvy riots to take place in Kent occurred at Cowden and Edenbridge in August 1866. As was often the case with these events, it was sparked off by jealousy and rivalry amongst the navvies themselves. The navvies were working on the Surrey & Sussex railway, which now forms the line from Edenbridge to Tunbridge Wells and Uckfield. The railway was being constructed by French engineers, Waring Bros., who had begun the works by employing English labourers at eight shillings per day. This was a high rate to pay and it was not long before the Warings began to import cheaper labour from abroad. Men from France, Luxembourg and Belgium were found who were prepared to work for wages of between 2/4d and 4/- per day, with the result that the English labourers began to be put out of work.

When the numbers of foreign workers had reached four or five hundred, the simmering anger of the English boiled over. They determined to drive off these invaders who were undercutting their own wages. The rioting started at 10.30 p.m. on a Sunday night, when the English gathered *en masse* at a place called Blower's Hill, near Cowden. From there they marched to the navvy camp at Markbeech, where a tunnel was being built, carrying bludgeons, staves and a whole assortment of dangerous implements. The navvies at Markbeech were mostly French; they were violently driven out and their huts demolished by the irate English. At first the French were inclined to put up a fight and some of them drew knives, but when they realised how outnumbered they were they fled in the direction of Edenbridge.

The English pursued them into Edenbridge and by Monday morning the town was effectively in the hands of the marauding navvies who were still lusting for French blood. Fortunately the Kent Constabulary had had time to react by then and some sixty or seventy Police had arrived to separate the English and foreign groups. The Chief Constable also took the precaution of sending for a hundred troops from Shorncliffe Camp. Had the forces of law and order not been able to assert themselves there might well have been a real bloodbath in the streets of Edenbridge; as it was, there were some twenty to thirty injuries and ten navvies were eventually charged.

One of the reasons why this incident did not boil over into something more serious was the speed with which the forces of law and order were able to react. This was due partly to the use of the electric telegraph and, most significantly, to the opportunity for rapid movement of men by railway as a result of the labours of previous groups of navvies. These two developments meant that riot was far less frequent in Kent as the century drew on; technology had come to the rescue.

5 Hop-Picker Riots

Every year a large number of migrant workers flocked into Kent to assist with the picking of the hops. Like the navvies, they endured poor conditions and hard work, as well as often being unpopular with local residents. Most of them came from London and included women and children as well as men, so were generally not regarded as being in the same league as the navvies when it came to riotous behaviour. Nonetheless there was often trouble with the hop-pickers, particularly at the end of the season in October. A few selected incidents will serve to illustrate the problem.

Tension between local villagers and the visiting hop-pickers was behind two violent incidents in 1866. On 10th August 1866 there was a battle between a group of Irish hop-pickers and the residents of Hadlow, the first round of which resulted in victory for the local 'team' when the Irish fled. However, the hop-pickers returned later that evening with an assortment of weapons causing the villagers to run off. This left the three local policemen facing a group of about thirty seething Irishmen, as a result of which the police were dealt a severe beating.

An incident a few weeks later at Ide Hill proved far more serious. 1866 had in fact been a bad year, with several strikes by hop-pickers and a lot of tension between them and the local people. One group of pickers from Surrey were working for a farmer at Toy's Hill near Brasted and had been lodging with a beerhouse keeper at Ide Hill named Joseph Leigh. It was traditional at the end of the season for the hop-pickers to reward their 'binman', if he had been helpful to them, and so the pickers went to Leigh's house for a few drinks and 'a bit of fun'. They left peacefully enough at 10 p.m, but were already in a fairly intoxicated state. Whilst wandering around they came across the 'Cock Inn', where more drinking took place. It would seem that the visitors were not popular with the landlord, nor with some of the local drinkers, and they were ordered out. No sooner were they outside than a fight started, in which at least three local men were involved, as a result of which a hop-picker named Dobson died.

The Police were called and, after a search, a hedge-stake was found in a local garden – this was undoubtedly the weapon that had finished off poor Dobson. A manslaughter verdict was reached against a local man and it seems quite certain that the locals had deliberately provoked a fight against pickers who they knew were incapacitated by drink.

Getting the hop-pickers out of Kent at the end of the season seems to have caused enormous problems for the local Police and also for the South Eastern Railway Company. The process was rarely accomplished without some unpleasant incident. A typical minor incident occurred at the 'Victory' pub in Barming during September 1873. A large group of people had gathered for a few drinks before setting off for the station, amongst them being John White. What exactly happened was clouded in everyone's memory by the copious consumption of alcohol, but it would seem that for some reason White was attacked by a number of people. In an effort to defend himself he lashed out with an earthenware quart pot (thereby providing an indication of the quantity of drink involved) which smashed against the head of a woman named Margaret McCarthy, cutting her cheek. White was handed over to the Police, which in itself shows that he must have been unpopular with the other hop-pickers. He was charged with unlawful wounding, but was found not guilty on the grounds that he had been defending himself and could not see who he was hitting due to the press of the crowd.

Most incidents of this type occurred in the Barming, Maidstone and East Farleigh region because these were the points where the hop-pickers assembled for their return journeys to London. In October 1874 a local reporter went to East Farleigh station to witness the strange exodus and provided a vivid account of the events – nearly all the participants in which were in some stage of intoxication. Large numbers of Police were on hand to filter the pickers through the ticket office a few at a time, otherwise they would all have made a charge for the train or forced their ways into the station building. The lining up made the crowd very restless and the filing through irritated them:

> 'This process goes on, much to the indignation of the mob, who would much prefer, with their characteristic impulsiveness, to block themselves into an immovable mass in the interior, until a sufficient number of tickets has been issued to fill the approaching train.'

The monotony of queuing was of course broken up by the hop-pickers' own form of entertainment – a few drunken brawls. At one point the reporter was alarmed to witness the breaking out of a free fight which mostly involved women and which included a lot of 'most unmerciful scratching and hair pulling'. Most fights like this were caused by the exchange of abuse or arguments over men.

As the engine and train steamed up towards the station platform, which was crammed with people, one drunken man fell off the platform and collapsed across the tracks in a completely insensible state; he was rescued in the nick of time by an alert Superintendent of Police. The arrival of the train was the cue for a pitched battle between everyone on the platform, the aim of which was to secure a seat. As the crowded train was pulling out another hop-picker fell from the platform beneath its wheels, receiving severe injuries to the thigh from which he died later that day. The reporter was astonished to notice that the other hop-pickers made no attempt to rescue their colleague, but left it all to the Police.

Similar scenes took place at the South Eastern Railway station in Maidstone, though the arrangements were slightly better. A special wooden ticket office was erected in the goods yard, protected with an array of barriers. The railway staff locked themselves into the building at the start of the day and barricaded the door from the inside with iron bars; they clearly did not relish their task! As the hop-pickers filed through to purchase their tickets, numerous attempts were made to defraud the railway staff – the most common method being to allege some short-changing or similar deceit by the SER men. Such was the volume of trade that £80 was collected in half an hour.

Crime did not cease when the hop-pickers had finally boarded the trains. Stories abounded in the local press and at least some of them may have had a grain of truth. It was said that one woman died in the course of the journey back to London and that her corpse was robbed of her eighteen shillings savings. Another report alleged that one woman had assaulted another on the train by bashing her head with a salt cellar. It was also rumoured that, after the return of the hop-pickers, the Irish areas of London were plunged into a state of complete drunkenness for several days.

Altogether it must be said that the hop-pickers posed a considerable challenge to the maintenance of law and order in Victorian Kent!

CHAPTER NINE

THE SMUGGLERS

1 The State of the Art

The heyday of the Kent smuggler occurred some time before Victoria ascended the throne; some would say that the smugglers were at their most powerful in the 1740s, when the notorious Hawkhurst Gang held sway over much of central Kent, on one famous occasion in 1747 launching a full-scale attack on the town of Goudhurst. But by the 1830s the smugglers were a poor lot, content with running the occasional load of brandy or tobacco across the Channel.

Nonetheless smuggling still had a romantic reputation which attracted the attention of the press. It had become a small-scale, and therefore more secretive, business, so local editors found it quite difficult to satisfy their readers' demands for interesting smuggling stories. A lot of rumours were printed, many of which were based merely on conjecture.

In about 1839 there was reckoned to be a considerable trade in illicit brandy across the Channel from France. Rumour had it that all sorts of fanciful ideas were employed to deceive the watchful customs men, including hollow masts into which the brandy could be poured. The whole trade was reckoned to be organised by a Jew named 'Buffy', but it was more likely that a number of local fishermen were merely supplementing their incomes. In October 1839 several barrels of brandy were found in suspicious circumstances at Boulogne, disguised with plaster of Paris to look like lumps of chalk. A gang of Dover smugglers was caught when a bragging smuggler told his sweetheart all about his nocturnal activities; she passed the information on to another man, whom she preferred to the smuggler, and several arrests were made.

Smuggling also took place along the Thames and Medway estuaries as well as along the Channel coast. In 1840 the barge *John of Maidstone* was stopped whilst off Milton, near Gravesend. Customs officials boarded the vessel and were informed that a cargo of iron was being carried. One of the officials threw off the tarpaulin that covered the load and exclaimed, 'This is pretty iron!' He had found a very considerable stock of smuggled spirits, amounting to over nine hundred gallons. There were 465 gallons of brandy, 159 gallons of cognac and 318 gallons of 'Geneva spirits'. There were also four chests of tea. Some of the crew attempted to escape by running across the marshes but they were soon caught and all involved were sent to prison.

Smuggled goods were discovered by chance at Margate in 1846. A cave on the beach was in use by a lime-burner, but at the back of it some barrels of alcohol had been concealed by sinking them into a pool of water. The case involved quite a lot of public interest since the cave was very close to the local Coastguard station and belonged to the solicitor to the Treasury – though he was not implicated in the smuggling.

Kent smuggling throughout the century consisted of numerous small cases like this, with the methods employed varying slightly. Towards the end of the century, for example, a man was caught whilst attempting to smuggle Turkish tobacco through the Customs at Dover. He had concealed it inside the tyres of his bicycle.

There was, however, one smuggling incident that aroused wider interest.

2 The Wouldham Smugglers, 1843

Smuggling was generally a communal affair, involving small groups of men who worked together or who lived in the same village. There can seldom, however, have been a case quite like that of the Wouldham smugglers where virtually an entire community was involved in the illegal trade.

In the winter of 1843 some customs officers who worked along the River Medway learnt that a consignment of French brandy was being brought in to Wouldham, where it was to be stowed away in secret. A group of Customs men therefore arrived in the village at about nine o'clock at night, confident that they would be able to catch the smugglers in the act. Instead they found a most unpleasant mob waiting for them: there were some sixty or seventy angry villagers, including bargees, limeburners and local tradesmen, blocking the street and armed with bludgeons and pitchforks. The angry mob was led by a drunken man later identified as Baker, a butcher from Rochester.

The Customs men were clearly outnumbered, so one of the officials appealed for help to the local Constable, Featherby, who was at the scene. Instead of helping the Customs men, Featherby incited the mob to attack them and showed the way by promptly assaulting two of the officials. Giving one of them a smart blow, Featherby said 'It's all in friendship', then he and the mob drove the frightened officials out of the village and back towards Rochester.

The officials took the only action now open to them and summoned the military. In due course two officers and seventeen men arrived from Chatham Barracks and the combined force entered the village. The opposition rapidly dispersed, allowing the Customs men to make a search. Their time had not been wasted, for they discovered 203 tubs of brandy in the cellar of Thomas Hart's beer shop, six tubs in a ditch and another four in a nearby field. A search of nearby houses uncovered another eleven tubs, making a total of 224 tubs worth over £1,000. A number of men were subsequently tried and found guilty, including the Rochester butcher, but for some reason none was punished.

CHAPTER TEN

THE POOR LAW AND THE NEW BASTILLES

1 The Relief of Poverty

As has already been noted, a large number of crimes were connected with poverty and the fear of incarceration in the workhouse. To understand why this should happen, it is necessary to know a little about the system for helping the poor.

The most common system of poor relief in Kent during the early 1800s was that of 'Outdoor Relief', based broadly on the Speenhamland system that had originated in Berkshire. Under this system a poor person could apply to the Relieving Officer or local magistrate of the Parish for financial assistance. The law was very strict on the matter and wandering beggars, for example, were unlikely to be received kindly. A man who abandoned his wife and children, so that the Parish had to pay for their upkeep, was also likely to be prosecuted since the cost of supporting his family would have to be paid by other local people out of taxation.

In 1834 the New Poor Law was passed. This allowed groups of Parishes to form together as a 'Union' and to build a workhouse for the provision of 'Indoor Relief'. The basic idea was only to provide relief inside a workhouse, so to discourage lazy people from claiming assistance. Conditions provided inside the workhouse were to be less pleasant than anything the lowest paid worker could expect outside.

In practice this new system never entirely worked. For a start there were never enough workhouses to cater for all the poor people and so the old and new systems tended to blend together somewhat. Also the poor were generally terrified of the workhouses, which were labelled the 'New Bastilles', and many had to be absolutely desperate before they would consider surrendering their freedom. Incidents like the Thom affair showed how inflamed opinion was on the subject and, in parts of Britain, feelings ran so high that the New Poor Law was never fully introduced.

Poverty forced people into breaking the law in a large number of ways. Begging and 'mendicity' were criminal offences. In April 1840 six men and a woman assembled at the tile kilns of a Mr Hart at Boughton under Blean. They demanded charity, but Mr Hart ordered them to go away. They did not take kindly to this and assaulted Hart before leaving. It was therefore not surprising that the residents of rural districts regarded any wandering persons with suspicion.

If a man abandoned his family it added expense to the local rates and so the authorities would often go to considerable lengths to apprehend the absconding husband. In Autum 1864 Isaac Diprose brought his family down to Cranbrook for the hop-picking, but in October ran off with all the money they had earned

– leaving his wife and children destitute. The abandoned family were taken into Cranbrook Union workhouse, then a hunt for Diprose began. Superintendent Smith received information that he had been seen in Devizes, Wiltshire, and travelled down to investigate. There he indeed found Diprose, who had taken work as a bricklayer. The wicked man was sentenced to three months' hard labour.

The workhouses themselves were often in the news, whether for the misdemeanours of the inmates or the 'masters', the men who ran them. As will be shown below, there were a number of cases of workhouse masters being prosecuted for cruel or indecent behaviour and a number were dismissed. In 1844, for example, the master of the Blean Union workhouse was dismissed for 'gross inhumanity'. A number of petty offences ended up in court as well, a youth called Woodcomber was given fourteen days' hard labour after he had been seen coming over the wall of the female section at the Tonbridge Union workhouse at three o'clock in the morning. Nearly all workhouses attached great importance to keeping male and female apart.

In February 1848 Canterbury had the unusual sight of twenty-one members of the workhouse in dock at the same time. After prayers one evening they had vowed to 'do for' the master and a riot had ensued. During the course of this the paupers had broken up one of the workhouse benches, which they had stuffed up a chimney and set on fire; this had nearly caused the whole building to be destroyed. In the end the Police had had to be called in to restore order. Hard labour was the reward for the paupers.

The workhouse inmates had very few opportunities to express their frustration at the treatment they received. One attempt by a workhouse inmate from Tunbridge Wells to protest landed her in court in 1839:

> 'Elizabeth Fry, charged with destroying a pair of unmentionables, was discharged upon a promise of future good behaviour.'

The workhouse did nothing to solve the problem of wandering beggars, in fact it probably made things worse by encouraging people to travel around looking for work. Some, however, virtually made a full-time occupation out of begging. One such man was Walter Scott, who appeared at Bearsted in 1874 charged with destroying a blanket whilst in Maidstone Gaol. He received ten days hard labour for this, but when released took up begging again and was soon 'charged with being a rogue and a vagabond' at Sutton Valence. It appeared that Scott had been touring the villages equipped with a letter intended to stir the sympathy of the public by claiming that he was deaf and dumb; his deception was not very effective since he kept breaking into speech as he had forgotten that he was meant to be dumb. On this occasion he was awarded twelve months hard labour to help him remember his mistakes.

2 The Hoo Union Workhouse Monster, 1841

The position of workhouse master afforded a man considerable opportunity for freedom of action. In theory he should have been subject to two higher tiers of management: the Poor Law Guardians, who were a body of local men responsible for that Union, and the Poor Law Commissioners, who were a central body based in London. In practice a master was usually free to do as he liked, particularly if he kept the burden on the local rates as low as possible.

James Miles, the master of the Hoo Union workhouse, had been exploiting this situation and had developed a sadistic streak. In 1838 his actions had come to the attention of Rev Pearson of Stoke, who heard that Miles had kept a girl shut up for seventy-two hours. However, the local Guardians were uninterested and so Miles was allowed to continue his evil practices until he appeared before the Magistrates in January 1841.

Miles was charged with cruelty and indecent assault involving five children – four girls and a boy. The case aroused considerable interest, especially as some of the children involved appeared in court to testify against Miles. It was commonly believed that Miles had made a habit of flogging children, including one of only two years old. Another rumour said that he had beaten a girl across the arms with a poker.

At least three girls provided vivid accounts of Miles' cruelty. Sarah Barnes, aged eleven, reported that he had laid her across a table, pulled up her petticoats and flogged her. She said that she had seen Miles flog other girls, making them take off all except their chemise and petticoat. Elizabeth Screes, aged twelve, stated that she had been stripped and flogged on her naked back with a birch rod. Jemima Dawes told the court that 'I was flogged by Mr Miles on the bare lower part of my person . . . I received about thirty stripes each time on my back'.

Miles admitted that some of the punishments he had used involved 'indelicate exposure', but despite all the evidence of cruelty the Poor Law Guardians had refused to prosecute Miles or to dismiss him.

The Magistrates remanded Miles on bail until the next Assizes. At the end of January 1841 Edwin Chadwick, the Secretary of the Poor Law Commissioners, wrote to say that Miles had been unwise and that the Commissioners wished him to be removed from his position. Yet still the Hoo Union refused to sack him. In April 1841 the Commissioners had to order his dismissal.

Miles was finally punished in March 1842, when he was given six months in prison.

3 The Milton Workhouse Libel Case, 1874

As will be noted from the public reaction to the Hoo case, not everyone favoured the workhouse system which tended to punish people for being poor without assisting them to find a better condition of life.

Thus it was that in 1874 a pamphlet began to circulate in the district around Milton, near Sittingbourne, written by a man using the pen-name of 'A Dreamer'. In fact the author was Rev. William Harker, the vicar of Milton, in whose Parish was situated the Milton Union workhouse where the master was John Kent. In the pamphlet the 'Dreamer' described various visions that he had seen; these included a vision of a poor, old man being forced to work on a treadmill, a road

Rev. Harker's Vision

lined with drops of blood and a sighting of a cross-bones. When Kent saw the pamphlet he was scandalised, believing it to be an attack on the way he ran the workhouse. In particular he alleged that the pamphlet was accusing him of cheating the local Guardians and of profiting by being cruel to the poor. Kent promptly accused Rev. Harker of libel and the case was heard in July 1874.

It was immediately clear that Rev Harker had the support of the inmates of the workhouse and many local people, so he determined to make a fight of it by claiming to be innocent of libel on the grounds that the accusations he had made were true. This was a rather risky course to take, especially as some of his charges against Kent were hard to prove. In particular he had accused the workhouse master of corruption, alleging that several mysterious parcels which had been taken from the workhouse to New Brompton station had contained pork which should have been fed to the paupers; instead, the clergyman believed, the master was selling it for his own profit and thereby deceiving the Poor Law Guardians who had paid for it.

Both Kent and Harker produced paupers to provide evidence. Several former paupers testified that Friday night dinners in the workhouse had consisted of potato mashed up with the peelings and soup that 'warn't soup at all'. Ellis, a former pauper, said that children had been forced to eat the skimmings from the coppers in which the food was cooked. Kent countered all this by producing several paupers who told the court that they were well fed and treated kindly; being inmates of the institution, however, they may not have been completely free agents in the matter.

Specific instances of the ill-treatment of paupers were also given. A rumour was reported that a woman named Esther Combes had been made to scrub floors only two days after she had given birth. It was usual at this time for people who needed medical attention but could not afford to pay for it to use the workhouse infirmary; one such instance of this was a man named Bowrey. Jane Bowrey, his widow, told the court that her husband had been sent to the workhouse infirmary at Christmas, 1872. He returned to her two weeks later in a state worse than when he had gone away, was put in Chatham hospital but died soon afterwards. Before dying, he told his wife that at the workhouse he had been made to sit in a cold place and clean potatoes in cold water under threat of being sent to prison if he refused. A Rainham surgeon gave evidence that Bowrey had been incapable of any work at the time of the incident.

Despite all this evidence the case went against Rev. Harker and he was found guilty of libel. Kent was awarded damages of £500, a very considerable amount for the time.

After the trial there remained a good deal of sympathy for Rev. Harker and the villagers of Milton began a fund in his support. However those who had the greatest sympathy for him were the poorest in society and the fund made slow progress; it had accumulated a mere £35 by December 1874.

CHAPTER ELEVEN

SOME UNUSUAL CRIMES

1 The Canterbury Spy Case, 1894

Some events seem so strange that it is difficult to believe them and on occasion this was so with matters that came up in the courts. One of the strangest cases in Victorian Kent concerned a man named Arthur Heath, who was arrested in Canterbury in 1894 and charged with being a wandering lunatic. He was locked up in the Canterbury workhouse for a while, then in June 1894 he was brought before the Magistrates who had to decide what to do with him. There he came out with a most amazing story, which the Magistrates apparently believed in its entirety.

Heath claimed that he was an officer in the United States armed forces. He told them that he had been on a mission that had involved travelling to London, but there he had been drugged and robbed. He said that he had lost a sum of money and some valuable papers. Whilst still in a stupefied state, due to the drugs, he had been put on board a train by the criminals, and had ended up in Canterbury because that was where the train terminated.

The Magistrates appear to have believed him, possibly because there were many spy stories circulating at the time. Such was their sympathy for Heath that they decided to give him thirty shillings from the poor box, which he used to pay his train fare out of the district. Perhaps they should have checked with the American embassy first!

2 The Shorne Witch, 1894

A most unusual assault case came before the Magistrates in 1894, involving two elderly residents of Shorne. The plaintiff, 86-year-old George Vulgar, alleged that Mary Murrell had hit him with a stick, but more sensationally he claimed that she was a witch!

Vulgar said that she had been causing him trouble for some time, but now had cast a most unpleasant spell on him. He claimed that she had been to Strood and got some 'stuff', which she burnt at midnight. This caused a red and blue light to burn before his eyes, in which he could see demons. He also claimed that one night she had burnt a tub of bumble bees in her room, as a result of which they had swarmed all night around the poor oid man.

George Vulgar did not explain how he reckoned to know so much about what happened in Mary Murrell's room at night, for the Magistrates regarded the whole business as plainly ridiculous and dismissed the case immediately.

3 Attacks on Railway Trains

It is one of Man's tendencies to imagine that things are always getting worse and that, somehow, in the past everyone was much better. One instance that is cited is that of vandalism, it being believed that this is a 20th century disease. In fact vandals have been alive and well for hundreds of years and with the dawn of the Victorian era were presented with a new target for their malicious energies – the railway train.

One of the first instances of an attack on a train took place at Higham, early in 1846. A man was standing on the overbridge near to Higham station, at the point where the railway from Gravesend to Strood ran alongside the Thames & Medway Canal. The man threw a stone down on a passing train, an action which the court interpreted as a deliberate attempt to derail the train into the canal. In his defence the man claimed that he was merely looking over the bridge when 'the stone fell from my hand'. This lame excuse impressed no-one, and he was given six months hard labour.

In July 1846 a charge of 'endangering a railway train' was brought against six boys in Canterbury, following what can only be described as a very determined and malicious attempt to do some damage. The six boys had got onto the Canterbury to Whitstable line of the South Eastern Railway on 12th July 1846 and had placed a series of obstacles along one and a half miles of track in a concerted attempt to cause a derailment. The obstacles included a four foot long iron bar, which was placed perpendicularly between the rails. Luckily an alert engine driver spotted the danger just in time and managed to stop his train by reversing the engine. The boys were caught since they were watching out to see what happened. Each was given three months hard labour.

A more unusual way of damaging a railway train was the fault of John Humphrey, a groom, who committed his offence at Bromley Common in 1865. Humphrey threw a live terrier over a bridge as a Ludgate to Dover express train was passing beneath. The animal smashed into the guard's compartment of one of the carriages; this had a glass 'observatory' or birdcage section for the guard to look out of, and this received a direct hit from the dog. Guard John Wells was knocked out by the impact and his face cut by glass. When he came to, Wells found the dead body of the terrier on the floor of his compartment. Humphrey was arrested and sent for trial at West Kent Sessions.

Such 'attacks' continued throughout the Victorian era, mostly involving small boys. In December 1894 two boys from New Brompton were typically charged with 'intent to injure a certain engine' of the London, Chatham & Dover Railway by throwing stones down its funnel. Not all the stones landed in the right place, since one seven pounder struck the tender of a passing goods train. The two boys received eight strokes of the birch each.

4 Offences Against Animals

During the early part of the period very little was thought about cruelty to animals, since it was a common practice and public sympathy was not aroused by it. However, by mid-Victorian times the subject had become a cause for concern and this led to the passage of the Cruelty to Animals Act. Under this legislation the RSPCA began to bring a number of prosecutions against individuals who had subjected animals to unnecessary suffering.

An early prosecution on this pattern followed some events that occurred near Bearsted in 1866. Some men gathered in a field near the village for some sport, which was planned to include sparrow shooting. One of them brought a tame cock in a bag. The poor creature's legs were tied together and it was fastened to the ground with a hazel rod across it. The owner of the bird then charged sixpence a time for people to shoot at it, finally selling its body for two shillings. The perpetrator of this deed was arrested, found guilty and given the choice of a £5 fine or two months in gaol.

A more bizarre event took place at the Medway Union workhouse in 1895. One of the inmates threw a cat at the night watchman, for which offence he was given twenty-one days hard labour.

A considerable legal tangle was involved in a Chatham incident of 1896. A couple called Lawrence were continually annoyed by a neighbour's cat which, not understanding the laws of trespass, kept straying into their garden. One further occasion proved too much for Henry Lawrence, who managed to capture the offending animal and threw it down his cess-pit. Some time later the woman who owned the cat came round to the Lawrence's house, having heard its plaintive cries from the cess-pit. When the woman told Mrs Lawrence that her cat was down their cess-pit, Mrs Lawrence responded in true vindictive manner: 'Oh yes it is. I had better put some water down and drown it'.

This seemed to be a simple case of cruelty to an animal – until the case arrived in court. It was revealed that, under the Cruelty to Animals Act, a stray dog could still be shot. The cat had clearly been trespassing and therefore, it was decided, could be treated in the same way as a stray dog. The case against the Lawrences was dismissed.

5 Highway Offences

It may be imagined that road traffic offences are something peculiar to the age of the internal combustion engine, but this is not so. In the Victorian era it was possible to break the road traffic laws in all sorts of bizarre ways.

One of the most common offences was 'furious driving'. This was a general term applied when a man was considered to be driving his horse and cart in such a way as to be a danger to the public. There were no official speed limits and the seriousness of the offence usually depended on the opinion of the Magistrates.

A rather more curious case took place in Tunbridge Wells in 1839. James Knowles was a fly-driver, virtually the equivalent of a taxi-driver today. His services were engaged by Sir James Gambier, who hired him at 2/6d per hour, but who soon became dissatisfied with Knowles' slow progress. Gambier told him to go faster, but Knowles simply threw down the reins and suggested that Gambier get out. Knowles was given fourteen days in prison for 'abandoning his fare'.

Drunken driving is a serious problem in the 1980s; it was also a cause for concern in Victorian Kent, though the results tended to be less frequently fatal than they are now. In early 1866 a Constable was patrolling the roads around

Chislet late in the evening when he was surprised to see a horse and cart approaching him in a most haphazard manner. The vehicle was wandering all over the road and it was clear that no-one was controlling the horse. The Constable climbed onto the cart and found a boy so deeply asleep that he had to be shaken vigorously before he could be awoken. The boy was only thirteen years old, but was nonetheless arrested and charged with driving a horse and cart on the turnpike road and 'being in such a position as to be unable to have the direction over the horse'. The boy claimed to have been 'drowsy', but the Magistrates suspected that drink had been involved and fined him 2/6d with 9/- costs.

6 Poaching

Poaching was a relatively common crime in the early part of Queen Victoria's reign and in many villages there was a silent battle of wits being played out between gamekeepers and poachers. Poaching was not always a crime that was motivated by profit; like sheep-stealing, it tended to tempt those of the poor who wanted a better meal for once. Chambers & Mingay, in their classic book *The Agricultural Revolution*, have observed that 'It was poverty and the longing for a taste of meat . . . which turned labourers into poachers and made the woods ring with nocturnal alarms'.

Poachers were generally solitary people, for they could operate more silently and efficiently that way. Sometimes, however, they ganged together – especially when they had to combat groups of gamekeepers. In the late 1830s a large gang, numbering up to thirty men, were a constant problem in the Cranbrook area: the *Maidstone Journal* referred to them as 'a gang of desperadoes who have long been a terror to this part of the county'.

When large numbers such as this were involved there was liable to be trouble, for a struggle in the darkness against a group of gamekeepers could involve untold violence. In March 1838 the Cranbrook poachers met in a beer-shop, where they blackened their faces with gunpowder and prepared their weapons. They proceeded into Blower's Hole Wood where they came up against a group of waiting gamekeepers; the poachers' first idea was to run, but when they discovered that they outnumbered the gamekeepers by thirty to eight they decided to fight instead. During the struggle a gamekeeper named Allchin received a cracked skull, from which he later died. Eleven of the poachers were eventually arrested and the four ringleaders were sent to Australia for fifteen years.

A few months later a similar violent incident took place at Cobham. In December 1838 gamekeeper Thomas Chipps was lying in wait for a poacher when he was surprised by four men. One of them – they were all poachers – named James Allen beat him about the head with the stock of the gun, then left him in the field to die. Allen evaded capture for a while, but was finally brought to trial in March 1840 – by which time one of his accomplices had already been transported for life. Allen was charged with the murder of Chipps and was also transported for life.

The Poaching Affray at Halling

One particularly notorious poacher was a rogue named Powell, who was active in parts of eastern Kent during the early 1840s. Powell was well-known because of the skill with which he evaded capture or with which he escaped from custody. In July 1843 he was arrested by the village Constable of Bridge, but managed to escape and was reputed to have run all the way to Canterbury wearing only a shirt! His next escapade came at Wingham in November 1843, where he was poaching when pounced upon by a gamekeeper named Brenchley. Powell struggled violently with the man, biting him and eventually managing to run off from Brenchley when the gamekeeper's wrist was strained. Brenchley's assistant, Booth, gave chase and the two men fought for twenty minutes, Powell managed to escape again by nearly biting through Booth's thumb. In December 1843 Powell was nearly caught again whilst poaching trout, but was finally captured at Charlton near Dover a few days later. Even on this last occasion he put up a struggle, using a knife and also helped by a woman who was with him.

At Halling in 1847 two gamekeepers were patrolling a wood well-known for its pheasants when they came across two men sitting by a fire. The two men claimed to be on their way from Sevenoaks to Maidstone, but said they had got lost. However, one of the gamekeepers recognised one of the men as being Silas Wood, a well-known poacher. It was the poachers who struck first, hitting out at the gamekeepers with the barrels of their guns. A furious struggle then began, which lasted forty-five minutes. Both sides used their guns as bludgeons and each grabbed the opponents by their neckerchieves, which had to be cut away. Wood managed to escape, but both men eventually appeared for trial. In court one of the poachers complained that a keeper had continually beaten his head against the ground and the Judge censured the gamekeepers for excessive violence. Both poachers were given two months' hard labour.

CHAPTER TWELVE

PUNISHMENT AND POLICE

Probably the most famous connection between Victorian Kent and the punishment of criminals was the prison hulks, old wooden warships moored on the Thames and the Medway that acted as disease-ridden floating prisons. The hulks and their convicts also featured in Charles Dickens' novel *Great Expectations.*

Strictly speaking the hulks were as much a part of Georgian as Victorian Kent since they ceased to be significant in 1856. The most important locations of the hulks were at Woolwich and Chatham. Hulks at Woolwich in 1837 included the *Justitia* and the *Ganymede* – a convict managed to escape from the latter in September 1837. To these was added the *Warrior*, which in 1841 held 638 prisoners in appalling conditions. There was also a hospital ship at Woolwich named the *Unité.*

There was a similar pattern on the Medway at Chatham, where from 1825 boys were imprisoned on the *Euryalus*. An old battleship, the *Cumberland*, was in use as a hulk at the beginning of the period and there was also the *Fortitude*. The hospital ship was named *Wye*.

A large number of the convicts on the hulks were men sentenced to transportation and so there were several desperate attempts at escape. Most of the convicts were handicapped by an inability to swim, common at the time, and so some ingenuity was needed in order to escape. In June 1838 seven dangerous characters from the *Fortitude* managed to steal a rowing boat and rowed across the Medway. Two of them were recaptured on Hoo Marshes and the rest near Wainscott. In January 1839 a convict named Thomas Moore escaped from the *Wye* with the assistance of a woman friend who had provided a boat. He was recaptured in Gravesend shortly afterwards.

The convicts from the hulks had their best chance of escape when they came ashore to work on tasks like stone-breaking. Men from the *Cumberland* did this every day, but all wore shackles and chains. On one occasion three did manage to escape in fog, but were soon caught again on Hoo Marshes.

The hulks, transportation to Australia and public hangings were the most unpleasant aspects of the legal system at the start of the Victorian era, but they were gradually swept away in a series of reforms. The hulks in Kent were finished with in 1856, but transportation lingered on. The use of transportation had been much reduced in 1841 and from 1853 it was employed only when a sentence of fourteen years or more was involved. The practice ceased in 1867. Public executions were stopped in 1868 (see Chapter One) and another unpleasant practice, that of imprisoning debtors, ceased in 1869.

Thus there was a generally liberal trend throughout the era, but this does not mean that the penal system became entirely enlightened. Sometimes the local policy differed from that of the Government, this being notably the case with the introduction of the Police. In 1843, for example, the Dover gaoler cropped the hair of two prisoners – a common practice fully approved of by the local Magistrates. Government policy under Peel disapproved of this practice and the Home Secretary directed the local Magistrates to read out a letter of censure to the gaoler. The latter resigned in disgust.

The tensions that could result under a repressive penal system were revealed by the trial of James Fletcher in 1866. Fletcher, a convict at Chatham, was accused of murdering prison warder James Boyle. Fletcher was in prison serving seven years penal servitude for robbery with violence and had been driven into a desperate state by the conditions there. He openly stated that he would rather die than endure any longer time in prison. Warder Boyle had reported Fletcher several times for poor discipline, as a result of which he had been confined to the cells. The warders had obviously marked him out as a troublemaker, since Fletcher claimed that the chief warder had threatened to 'make my head and the wall come together'. The murder occurred when Boyle and one other warder were supervising a gang of twenty convicts who were stone breaking in Chatham Dockyard. Fletcher attacked Boyle with the hammer given to him for breaking stones and struck the warder three times. At his trial Fletcher said that there was a man in the prison who was dying of starvation. He said that men were so hungry that they were eating candles, soap and tallow as well as drinking oil out of tins. Fletcher was sentenced to death in December 1866.

A lot can be learnt about the values of Victorian society by examining the punishments given for various crimes. Below is an example drawn from the West Kent Quarter Sessions, January 1838:

Offence	**Punishment**
Theft of one sheep	Fifteen years transportation
Theft of one donkey (value 30s.)	12 months hard labour
Theft of one rabbit and three towels	3 months in prison
Theft of two sheep skins	7 years transportation
Theft of two bushels of apples (value 6s.)	2 months hard labour
Theft of one pair of boots	3 months hard labour
Theft of pocket book (value 4d.) by servant who also slept in master's bed when away	4 months hard labour
Theft of one faggot (worth 4d.)	1 month hard labour
Theft of 15s. cash (by 14 yr. old boy)	7 years transportation
Theft of bacon (value 4d.)	2 months hard labour

Punishments for theft were generally severe, especially where a man's servant was involved. A Maidstone servant who stole a bushel of malt was transported for life in January 1837. Two other men got seven years' transportation for stealing a bullock's tongue from a butcher's shop in Maidstone.

Sometimes a straightforward theft was complicated by some other form of indiscretion liable to incur the Judge's wrath. William Hall stole two stockings, one coat, one handkerchief, two shoes and nine yards of cotton (total value 7/3d) from a man in Upchurch, but compounded his wickedness by eloping with the man's wife as well. He was given ten years' transportation in 1845.

The punishments for crimes of theft were gradually softened as the century wore on and this applied to some other crimes as well. The list below draws on events at the Kent Summer Assize, 1883:

Offence	**Punishment**
Theft of 1 lamb	12 months in prison
Theft of half a gallon of nuts and 2/-	3 months hard labour
Theft of silver watch and gold chain	4 months hard labour
Theft of coat (value £1)	18 months hard labour
Theft of pair of shoes	1 month hard labour
Theft of £4 household goods by Policeman	4 months hard labour
Burglary	18 months hard labour
Burglary and threats	9 months hard labour
Forging banker's cheques	7 years penal servitude
Assault on woman	7 years penal servitude
Perjury	4 months hard labour

One of the peculiarities of the penal system at the start of the era was that it was often more dangerous to steal a small item of property than to physically assault someone; crimes against property were considered more threatening to society than crimes against the body. By the end of the Victorian Age this situation was no longer quite so pronounced, but crimes of theft could still be punished severely even if they involved only small amounts; in 1895 a Chatham man was given 4 months hard labour for stealing three walking sticks.

In the early 19th century the maintenance of law and order was a local responsibility, the usual object of which was to spend as little as possible. Police forces emerged during the Victorian era as a result of Government legislation – London being far in advance of the rest of the country in this matter. Peel had set up the Metropolitan Police in 1829; from 1835 municipal corporations were instructed to form efficient constabularies and from 1839 the Counties were expected to do likewise. Many local people considered this an unreasonable intrusion into their affairs by central government and Kent proved to be one of the most dilatory Counties in this respect. In 1856 The County & Borough Police Act was passed which made provision of a Police Force compulsory and so a Kent Constabulary was finally formed on 14th January 1857. Many of the Kent Boroughs had equipped themselves with a Police Force some time before this, for example the Maidstone Police commenced duty in 1836.

During the late 1830s law and order was a hot issue in local politics. Different parties had different ideas on the subject; in Maidstone in 1835-6 the Tories spent £352 on policing, but in 1836-7 the Liberals spent £1,076. In 1837 the people of Chatham were demanding provision of a 'night patrol' since crime was so common and at the same time Gillingham, Brompton and Rainham began to arrange watching and lighting of streets on the rates.

Some men got impatient with waiting for the local authorities to do anything and developed their own ideas. In 1837 a Rochester butcher got so fed up with people stealing meat from his slaughterhouse that he attached a system of ropes and weights to a pistol. When a small boy entered the slaughterhouse the contraption exploded, so frightening the boy that he was easily caught.

In 1842 the people of Loose set up their own night patrol of five men, who were instructed to keep a strict watch 'over the haunts of ill-disposed characters'.

From 1857 the entire County was more effectively policed and the use of the military to help maintain law and order declined. The first detective branch of the County Force was formed in 1896, the same year that the first Police bicycles were issued.

Only one Policeman was murdered in Kent during the Victorian era. He was Constable Israel May, who was found dead at Snodland in August 1873. May had been battered to death with his own truncheon. A bloodstained cap and some broken braces were found nearby and these were traced to a certain Thomas Atkins who was arrested a few days later at Kingsdown. There was a history of mental illness in Atkins' family, his father having murdered his mother, and he was found guilty of manslaughter. The sentence was fifteen years penal servitude.

Policemen were often unpopular with local people and to be an effective Constable required skill and tact. An unusual attempt at revenge on an unpopular policeman occurred at Strood in 1894, when a woman claimed that a policeman was the father of her illegitimate child. When the case came up in court the woman was let down by her rather 'loose' reputation.

SOURCES

This book is based entirely on primary resources, most notably the Kent local newspapers of the period. I am most grateful to the staff of the libraries at Maidstone and Chatham for their help.

NOTES FOR SCHOOLS

A lot of the material in this book can be used as local history material either worth studying in its own right, or worth using as material to illustrate the widely used 'O' Level and CSE courses on British Social & Economic History. Apart from directly covering the theme of crime and punishment, this book can also be used to look at the position of women in society and to study the effects of the imposition of the New Poor Law in Kent.

Study Guide

It is suggested that this book is best studied along various themes. The sections of the book which apply to each theme are indicated with their chapter numbers.

Poverty and its Relief: 3iii, 8i, 10.

The best theme to pursue is that of how the poor people reacted to the New Poor Law, why they hated it so much, and what effect it had on public order in the County.

Motives for Crime: Derek Fraser has written that 'most nineteenth century crime was concerned with gain'. Was this true? Assess the importance of the various motives found in this book –

Hunger – 3iii, 10, 11vi
Revenge – 6
Economic interests – 8ii, 8iv
Personal profit – 3i, 3ii, 7iii, 9ii

Punishment of Criminals: 3, 12

Consider the way in which crimes were punished, comparing the penalties given to those whose crimes were against property and against person. Chapter One might also be used for comparison.

Maintenance of Public Order: 5, 6, 7ii, 7v, 8

Why did public order break down so frequently?

Themes to note – use of military, importance of electric telegraph, railways, organised Police.

Crimes that have vanished: examine why some crimes were common in the 1800s but have now disappeared. This may be due to decline of motive or more effective law enforcement, occasionally also due to changes in the law.

Highway robbery – 3ii
Sheep-stealing and poaching – 3iii, 11vi
Breach of promise – 4i
Prize fights – 7ii

Treatment of Lunatics: 1ii, 1iv, 1v, 7iv

Examine how attitudes to lunatics and the treatment of them have changed.

Women in Society: 4

Examine the problems and disadvantages of women in the Victorian era; why was prostitution so common. Recommended background reading: *The Dark Angel* by Fraser Harrison (Fontana).

Project Work

This material easily lends itself to project work by pupils outside of school and can allow them to research local history using primary resources with comparative ease. A project could examine, for example, crime in Kent over the course of one particular year. Most of the larger reference libraries have a collection of old local newspapers, generally on microfilm; access to the material is thus very simple.

INDEX OF PEOPLE

INDEX OF PLACES

Meresborough Books

Proprietors Hamish and Barbara Mackay Miller
7 STATION ROAD, RAINHAM, GILLINGHAM, KENT. ME8 7RS
Telephone Medway (0634) 371591

LARGE FORMAT PICTORIAL PAPERBACKS

THE MOTOR BUS SERVICES OF KENT AND EAST SUSSEX – A brief history by Eric Baldock. An illustrated history from 1899 to 1984 containing 146 photographs. ISBN 959. £4.95.

ROCHESTER FROM OLD PHOTOGRAPHS – see under hardbacks.

PEMBURY IN THE PAST by Mary Standen. ISBN 916. £2.95.

OLD MARGATE by Michael David Mirams. ISBN 908. £2.95.

OLD RAMSGATE by Michael David Mirams. ISBN 797. £2.95.

EXPLORING OLD ROCHESTER by John Bryant. A guide to buildings of historic interest. ISBN 817. £2.95.

THOMAS SIDNEY COOPER OF CANTERBURY by Brian Stewart. The life and work of Britain's best cattle painter, with 10 illustrations in colour. ISBN 762 £2.95.

A FIRST PICTUREBOOK OF OLD CHATHAM by Philip MacDougall. ISBN 754. £2.95.

A SECOND PICTUREBOOK OF OLD CHATHAM by Philip MacDougall. ISBN 924. £2.95.

CRANBROOK by Jenni Rodger. A pictorial history. ISBN 746. £2.95.

KENT TOWN CRAFTS by Richard Filmer. A pictorial record of sixteen different crafts. ISBN 584. £2.95.

KENTISH RURAL CRAFTS AND INDUSTRIES by Richard Filmer. A wide variety of rural crafts. ISBN 428. £2.50.

SMARDEN: A PICTORIAL HISTORY by Jenni Rodger. ISBN 592. £2.95.

A PICTURE BOOK OF OLD SHEPPEY by Michael Thomas. 130 old photographs, mostly from glass negatives. ISBN 657. £2.95.

FIVE MEDWAY VILLAGES by Wyn Bergess and Stephen Sage. A pictorial history of Aylesford, Burham, Wouldham, Eccles and Borstal. ISBN 649. £2.95.

A PICTURE BOOK OF OLD HERNE BAY by Harold Gough. 146 old pictures from the archives of the Herne Bay Record Society. ISBN 665. £2.95.

OLD SANDWICH by Julian Arnold and Andrew Aubertin. 146 old photographs. ISBN 673. £2.95.

AVIATION IN KENT by Robin Brooks. A pictorial history from 19th century ballooning to 1939. ISBN 681. £2.95.

A PICTURE BOOK OF OLD RAINHAM by Barbara Mackay Miller. ISBN 606. £2.95.

THE LIFE AND ART OF ONE MAN by Dudley Pout. A Kentish farmer's son who became successful as a commercial artist and as a children's illustrator. ISBN 525. £2.95.

OLD MAIDSTONE'S PUBLIC HOUSES by Irene Hales. 123 photographs. ISBN 533. £2.95.

OLD MAIDSTONE Vol. 1 by Irene Hales and Kay Baldock. ISBN 096. £2.50.

OLD MAIDSTONE Vol. 2 by Irene Hales. ISBN 38X. £2.50.

OLD ASHFORD by Richard Filmer. A photographic study of life in Ashford over 150 years. ISBN 72X. £2.95.

OLD TONBRIDGE by Don Skinner. ISBN 398. £2.50.

KENT TRANSPORT IN OLD POSTCARDS by Eric Baldock. 146 photographs. ISBN 320. £2.95.

GEORGE BARGEBRICK Esq. by Richard-Hugh Perks. The story of Smeed Dean Ltd in Sittingbourne and its colourful founder, George Smeed. 80 illustrations. ISBN 479. £2.95.

STANDARD SIZE PAPERBACKS

BIRDWATCHING IN KENT by Don Taylor. Details of when and where to watch for which birds, plus very readable accounts of personal experiences. ISBN 932. £4.50.

CRIME AND CRIMINALS IN VICTORIAN KENT by Adrian Gray. An insight into an intriguing if unsavoury side of Victorian life in Kent. ISBN 967. £3.95.

CHIDDINGSTONE – AN HISTORICAL EXPLORATION by **Jill Newton.** An enthusiastic account of this famous Tudor village. ISBN 940. £1.95.

STOUR VALLEY WALKS from Canterbury to Sandwich by Christopher Donaldson. Enjoy six days walking along the route taken by Caesar, Hengist & Horsa, St Augustine and many others. ISBN 991. £1.95.

THE GHOSTS OF KENT by Peter Underwood, President of the Ghost Club. ISBN 86X. £3.95.

CURIOUS KENT by John Vigar. A selection of the more unusual aspects of Kent history. ISBN 878. £1.95.

REAL ALE PUBS IN KENT by CAMRA in Kent. ISBN 894. £1.50.

A CHRONOLOGY OF ROCHESTER by Brenda Purle. ISBN 851. £1.50.

SITTINGBOURNE & KEMSLEY LIGHT RAILWAY STOCKBOOK AND GUIDE. ISBN 843. 95p.

A GUIDE TO HISTORIC KENT by Irene Hales. A guide to the most interesting features of every town and village, with details of each place of historic interest open to the public. ISBN 711. £1.50.

DOVER REMEMBERED by Jessie Elizabeth Vine. Personal memories from the early years of this century. ISBN 819. £3.95.

THE PLACE NAMES OF KENT – see under hardbacks.

PENINSULA ROUND (The Hoo Peninsula) by Des Worsdale. ISBN 568. £1.50.

A HISTORY OF CHATHAM GRAMMAR SCHOOL FOR GIRLS, 1907-1982 by Audrey Perkyns. ISBN 576. £1.95.

CYCLE TOURS OF KENT by John Guy. No. 1: Medway, Gravesend, Sittingbourne and Sheppey. ISBN 517. £1.50.

THE CANTERBURY AND WHITSTABLE RAILWAY 1830-1980: A PICTORIAL SURVEY. ISBN 118. 75p.

ROCHESTER'S HERITAGE TRAIL. (Published for The City of Rochester Society.) A useful guide for the visitor to most places of interest in Rochester. ISBN 169. £1.25.

WINGS OVER KENT. A selection of articles by members of the Kent Aviation Historical Research Society. ISBN 69X. £1.95.

LULLINGSTONE PARK: THE EVOLUTION OF A MEDIAEVAL DEER PARK by Susan Pittman. ISBN 703. £3.95.

LET'S EXPLORE THE RIVER DARENT by Frederick Wood. Walking from Westerham to Dartford. ISBN 770. £1.95.

SAINT ANDREW'S CHURCH, DEAL by Gregory Holyoake. ISBN 835. 95p.

BIRDS OF KENT: A Review of their Status and Distribution. A reprint, with addendum, of the 448 page study by the Kent Ornithological Society. ISBN 800. £6.95.

Further titles are in preparation. Details will be announced in 'Bygone Kent'.